AIN'T THAT A SHAME

Moderate swing ♩ = 120 (♫ = ♪³♪)

Words and Music by
ANTOINE DOMINO and DAVE BARTHOLOMEW

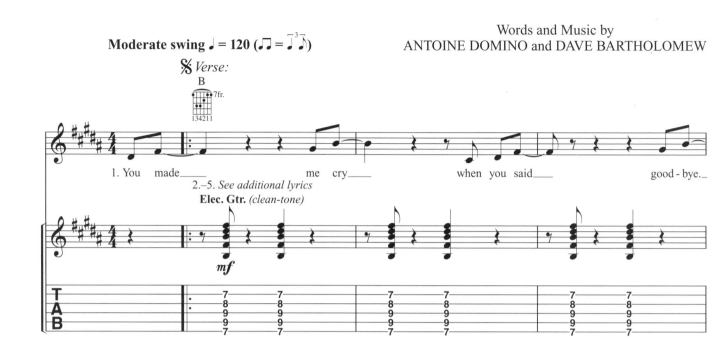

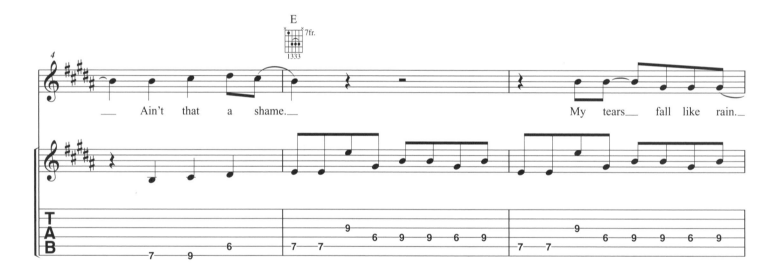

Ain't That a Shame - 3 - 1

Ain't That a Shame - 3 - 2

Verse 2:
You broke my heart
When you said we'll part.
Ain't that a shame.
My tears fell like rain.
Ain't that a shame.
You're the one to blame.

Verse 3:
Oh well, goodbye,
Although I'll cry.
Ain't that a shame.
My tears fell like rain.
Ain't that a shame.
You're the one to blame.
(To Sax Solo:)

Verse 4:
You made me cry.
When you said goodbye.
Ain't that a shame.
My tears fell like rain.
Ain't that a shame.
You're the one to blame.

Verse 5:
Oh well, goodbye,
Although I'll cry.
Ain't that a shame.
My tears fell like rain.
Ain't that a shame.
You're the one to blame.

AT LAST

Music by HARRY WARREN
Lyrics by MACK GORDON

ANOTHER SATURDAY NIGHT

Words and Music by
SAM COOKE

Verse 2:
Now, another fella told me,
He had a sister who looked just fine.
Instead of being my deliverance,
She had a strange resemblance
To a cat named Frankenstein.
Here…
(To Chorus:)

Verse 3:
It's a hard on a fella,
When he don't know his way around.
If I don't find me a honey
To help me spend my money,
I'm gonna have to blow this town,
Here it's…
(To Chorus:)

BABY IT'S YOU

Words and Music by
BURT BACHARACH, MACK DAVID
and BARNEY WILLIAMS

Baby It's You - 2 - 1

BODY AND SOUL

Words and Music by
RICK NOWELS and ELLEN SHIPLEY

Verse 2:
I've wasted too much time
Living for what wasn't mine.
And then came the day I found you.
And now I want nothing less,
I've found a love that's truly blessed.
And I wanna make my dreams come true.
(To Chorus:)

Body and Soul - 4 - 4

BOOGIE OOGIE OOGIE

Words and Music by
PERRY KIBBLE and JANICE MARIE JOHNSON

*Chord names represent overall harmony.

Boogie Oogie Oogie - 5 - 1

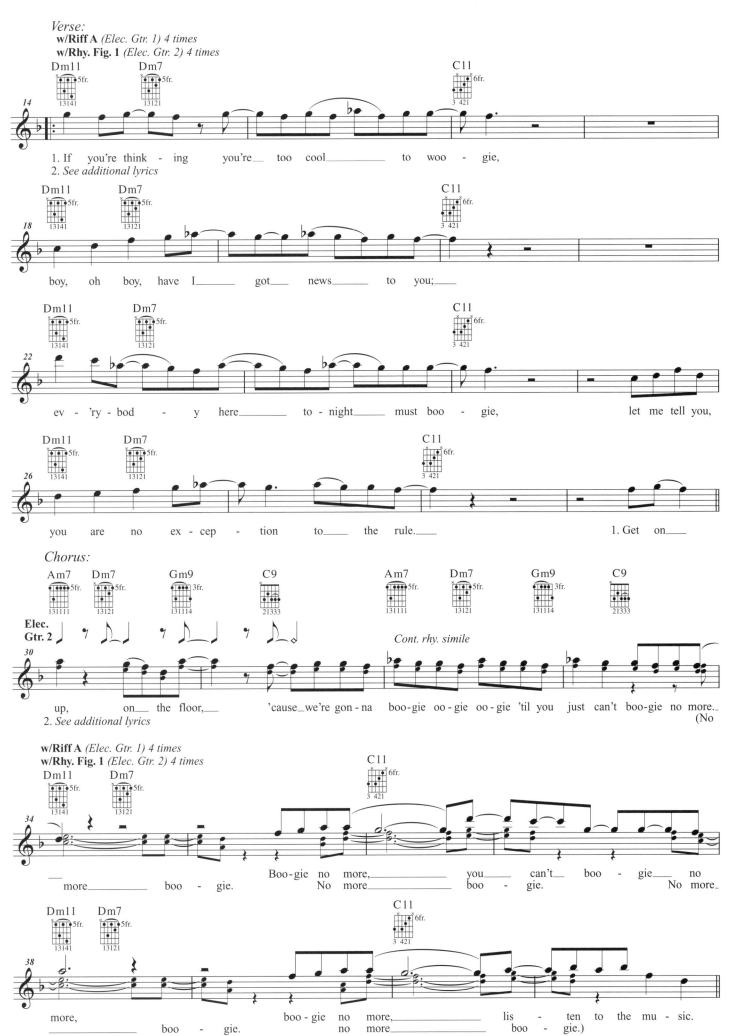

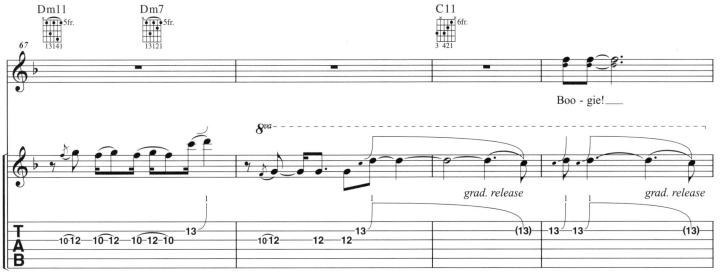

24

Verse 2:
There's no time to waste, let's get this show on the road.
Listen to the music and let your body flow.
The sooner we begin, the longer we've got to groove.
Listen to the music and let your body move.

Chorus 2:
Now get on up on the floor
Cuz we're gonna boogie oogie oogie.
Till you just can't boogie no more (boogie)
Boogie no more.
You can't boogie no more (boogie)
Boogie no more, listen to my bass here.
(To Bass Solo:)

Boogie Oogie Oogie - 5 - 5

CHAIN GANG

Words and Music by
SAM COOKE

Chain Gang - 3 - 1

Chain Gang - 3 - 2

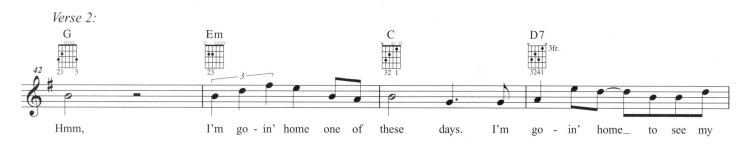

Verse 2:

Hmm, I'm go-in' home one of these days. I'm go-in' home_ to see my

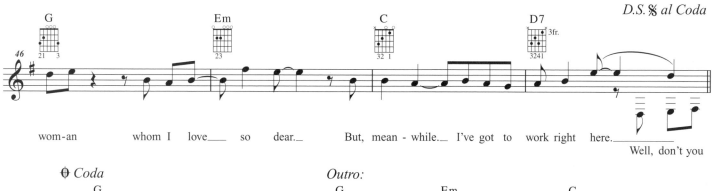

D.S. % al Coda

wom-an whom I love_ so dear._ But, mean-while._ I've got to work right here._ Well, don't you

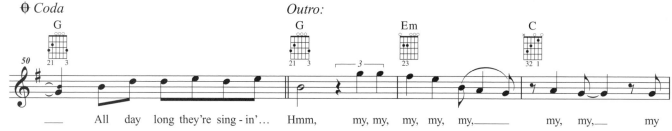

⊕ *Coda* *Outro:*

_ All day long they're sing-in'… Hmm, my, my, my, my, my,_ my, my,_ my

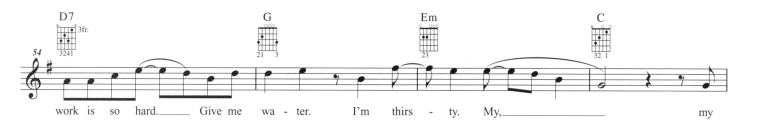

work is so hard._ Give me wa-ter. I'm thirs-ty. My,_ my

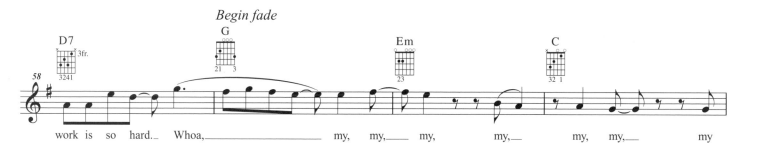

Begin fade

work is so hard._ Whoa,_ my, my,_ my, my,_ my, my,_ my

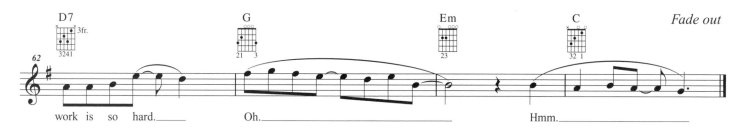

Fade out

work is so hard._ Oh._ Hmm._

Chain Gang - 3 - 3

BREEZIN'

Words and Music by
BOBBY WOMACK

*Chords reflect implied harmony.

Breezin' - 8 - 1

*Bass plays B.

Cont. rhy. simile

32

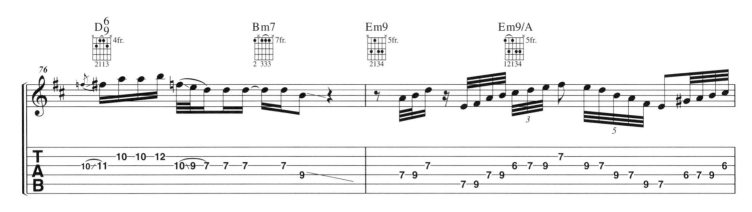

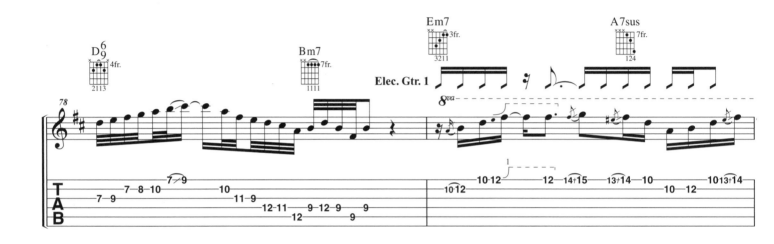

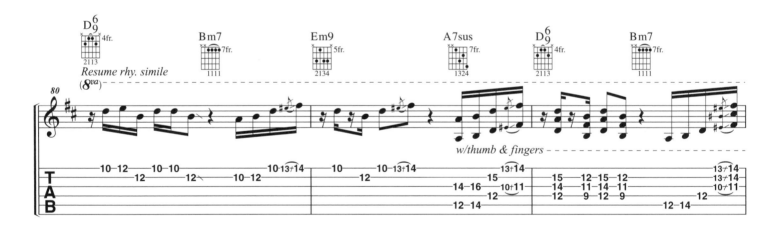

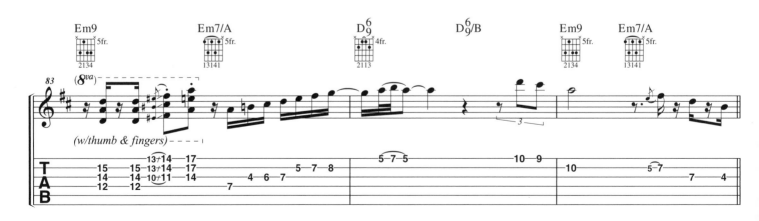

BRING IT ON HOME TO ME

Words and Music by
SAM COOKE

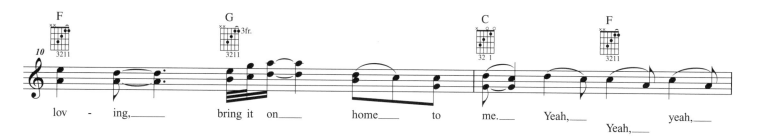

lov - ing,_____ bring it on___ home___ to me.___ Yeah,___ Yeah,___ yeah,___

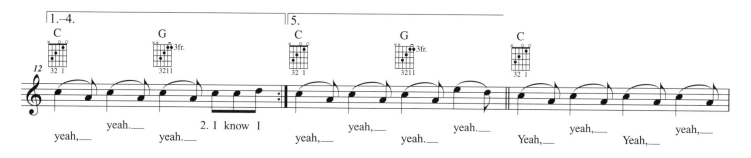

1.–4.

yeah,___ yeah.___ yeah.___ 2. I know I yeah,___ yeah.___ Yeah,___ yeah,___ yeah,___

5.

Fade out

Yeah,___ yeah,___ Yeah,___ yeah,___ Yeah,___ yeah,___ Yeah,___ yeah,___ Yeah,___ yeah,___ Yeah,___ yeah,___

Verse 2:
I know I laughed when you left.
But now I know I only hurt myself.
Baby, bring it me, bring your sweet lovin'.
Bring it on home to me, yeah, yeah, yeah.

Verse 3:
I'll give you jewelry, and money too.
That ain't all, that ain't all I'll do for you.
Baby, if you bring it me, bring your sweet lovin'.
Bring it on home to me, yeah, yeah, yeah.

Verse 4:
You know I'll always be your slave
'Til I'm buried, buried in my grave.
Oh, honey, bring it me, bring your sweet lovin'.
Bring it on home to me, yeah, yeah, yeah.
One more thing.

Verse 5:
I tried to treat you right
But you stayed out, stayed out in the night
But I'll forgive you, bring it to me, bring your sweet lovin'.
Bring it on home to me, yeah, yeah, yeah.
Yeah, yeah, yeah, yeah.
(Repeat and fade)

A CHANGE IS GONNA COME

Words and Music by
SAM COOKE

A Change Is Gonna Come - 2 - 1

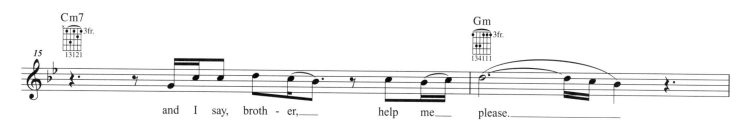

and I say, broth - er,___ help me___ please._____

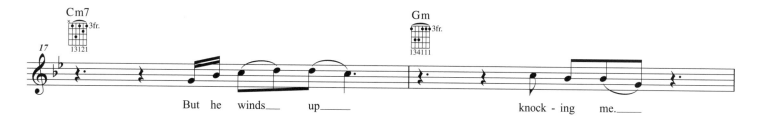

But he winds___ up_____ knock - ing me.____

D.S. % al Coda

back down on___ my_____ knees._____ Oh. 4. There've been

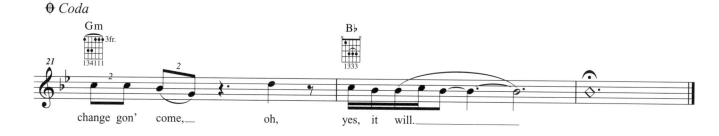

🔴 *Coda*

change gon' come,___ oh, yes, it will._____

Verse 2:
It's been too hard living but I'm afraid to die
'Cause I don't know what's up there beyond the sky.
It's been a long, a long time comin',
But I know, oh-oo-oh,
A change gon' come, oh, yes, it will.

Verse 3:
I go to the movie and I go downtown.
Somebody keep tellin' me don't hang around.
It's been a long, a long time comin',
But I know, oh-oo-oh,
A change gon' come, oh, yes, it will.
(To Bridge:)

Verse 4:
There've been times that I thought I couldn't last for long
But now I think I'm able to carry on.
It's been a long, a long time comin',
But I know, oh-oo-oh,
A change gon' come, oh, yes, it will.

CROSSFIRE

Words and Music by
KAL MANN and DAVID APPELL

Crossfire - 4 - 1

Repeat ad lib. & fade

Verse 2:
When they started doin' that crazy dance,
Well, that was the ruin of my big romance.

Chorus 2:
Got caught in the crossfire.
Crossfire, crossfire.
And I never ever had a chance.
I need you, baby.
(To Bridge:)

Verse 3:
I looked for my baby but he ain't in view.
I'm lookin' like crazy, what else could I do?

Chorus 3:
Can't boomed up crossfire.
Crossfire, crossfire.
And I found him when the dance was through.
I found my baby.
(To Bridge 2:)

CUPID

Words and Music by
SAM COOKE

Cu - pid, draw___ back your bow,___ and let your___ ar - row go___

straight to my lov - er's heart for___ me,___ { 1. for me.___ } { 2.3. no - bod - y but me.___ }

Cupid - 3 - 1

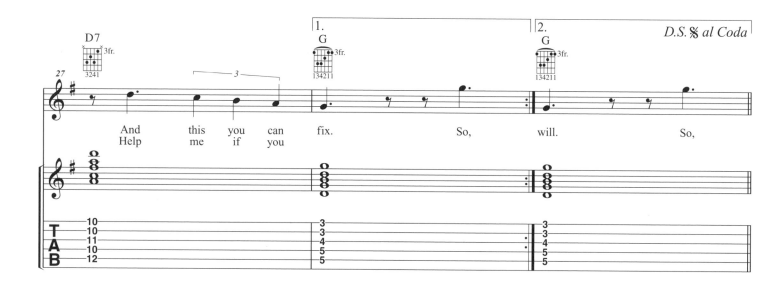

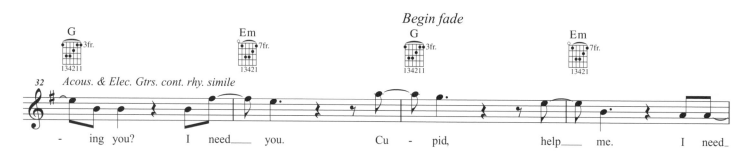

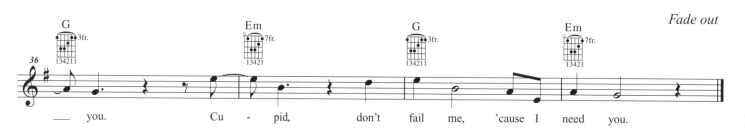

Cupid - 3 - 3

DISCO INFERNO

Moderately ♩ = 126

Intro:
Cm7

Words and Music by
LEROY GREEN and TYRONE KERSEY

*Chord names represent overall harmony.

Disco Inferno - 3 - 1

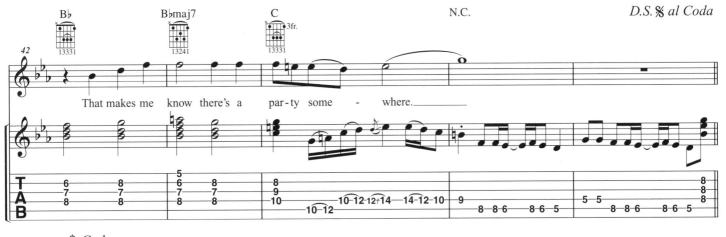

D.S. 𝄋 al Coda

That makes me know there's a par-ty some - where._____

⊕ Coda

w/Rhy. Fig. 1 (Elec. Gtr. 1) first 4 bars until fade

w/Fill 1 (Elec. Gtr. 2) on 1st repeat
w/Fill 2 (Elec. Gtr. 2) on 2nd repeat
w/Fill 3 (Elec. Gtr. 2) on 3rd repeat

Repeat and fade

_____ ba - by, burn! Dis-co in-fer - no! Burn,_ ba - by, burn! Burn the moth-er down! Burn,_

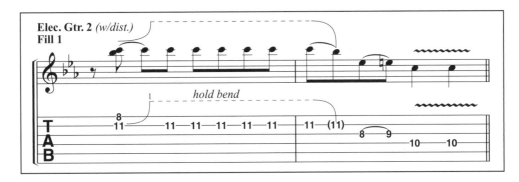

Elec. Gtr. 2 (w/dist.)
Fill 1

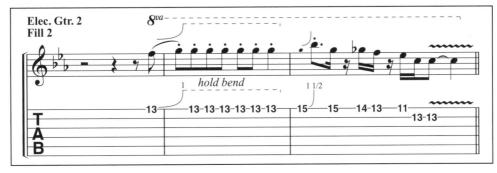

Elec. Gtr. 2
Fill 2

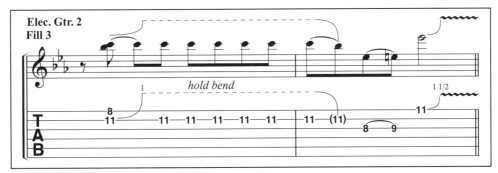

Elec. Gtr. 2
Fill 3

Verse 2:
Satisfaction came in a chain reaction.
(Burnin'.)
I couldn't get enough, 'til I had to self-destruct.
(Doo, doo, doo!)
The heat was on, rising to the top.
Everybody going strong, and that is when my spark got hot.
I heard somebody say…
(To Chorus:)

Verse 3:
Satisfaction came in a chain reaction.
(Let me hear.)
I couldn't get enough, so I had to self-destruct, mmm.
The heat was on, rising to the top, hmm.
Everybody going strong, and that is when my spark got hot.
I heard somebody say…
(To Coda)

Disco Inferno - 3 - 3

DRIFTIN' BLUES

Words and Music by
CHARLES BROWN, JOHNNY MOORE
and EDDIE WILLIAM

Driftin' Blues - 4 - 1

52

I'll__ be so__ far a-way.

Verse 2:
If my baby would only take me back again,
If my baby would only take me back again,
Well, you know I ain't good for nothin', baby,
Well, I haven't got no friends.
(To Guitar Solo:)

Verse 3:
I give you all my money; tell me what more can I do?
I give you all my money; tell me what more can I do?
Well, you just look good, little girl,
But you just won't be true.
(To Verse 4:)

EARTH ANGEL (WILL YOU BE MINE)

Moderately slow ♩. = 76

Words and Music by
JESSE BELVIN

Earth Angel (Will You Be Mine) - 3 - 1

Earth Angel (Will You Be Mine) - 3 - 2

Verses 3 & 4:

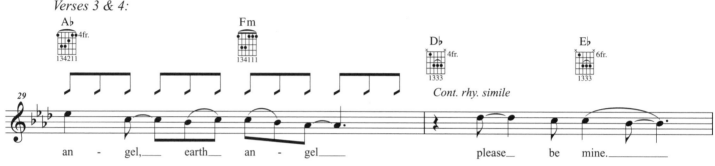

FLASHLIGHT

Words and Music by
GEORGE CLINTON, BOOTSY COLLINS
and BERNARD WORRELL

*Chord names represent overall harmony.

Now I lay me down to sleep.

Ooh, I just can't find the beat.

Flashlight - 5 - 1

58

Bridge:

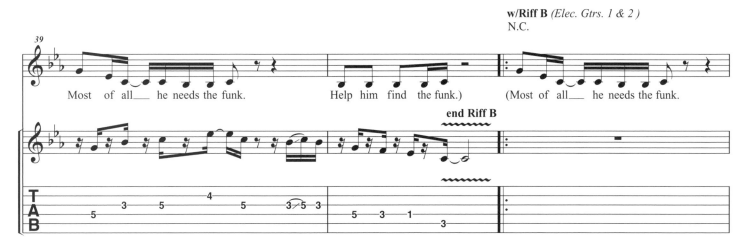

Play 2 times

FORGET YOU

Words and Music by
CHRISTOPHER BROWN, PHILIP LAWRENCE, ARI LEVINE,
BRUNO MARS and THOMAS CALLAWAY

Forget You - 4 - 1

GEORGY PORGY

Words and Music by
DAVID PAICH

*Chord frames are implied throughout.

Georgy Porgy - 5 - 1

68

Georgy Porgy - 5 - 3

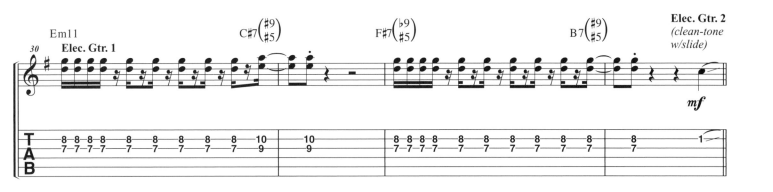

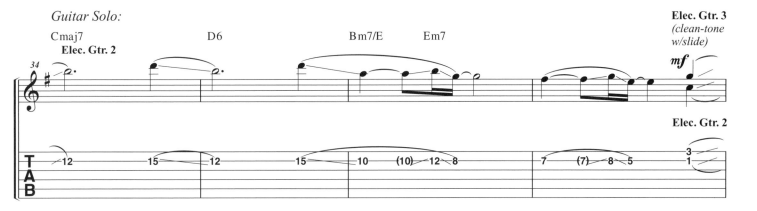

Guitar Solo:

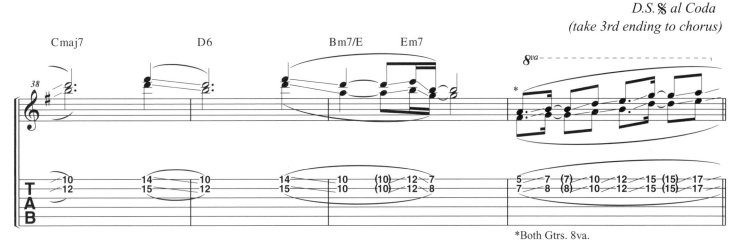

*Both Gtrs. 8va.

⊕ *Coda*

Geor - gy Por - gy, pud-din' pie,___ kissed the girls___ and made___ them cry.___

HERE WE GO AGAIN

Words and Music by
DAVID ROMANI, MAURO MALAVASI,
WAYNE GARFIELD, JERMAINE DUPRI,
TRINA BROUSSARD and LLOYD SMITH

Here We Go Again - 3 - 1

72

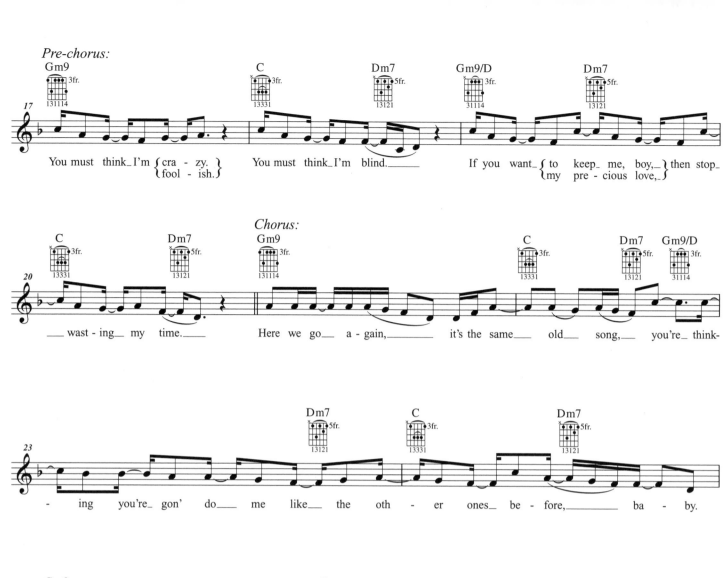

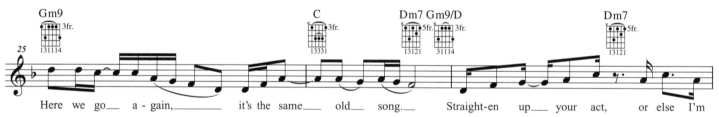

Here We Go Again - 3 - 2

so man - y times.___ So man-y times, you've mis - treat - ed__ me._____ Oh.__

Chorus w/ad. lib. vocals:

Here we go___ a - gain, it's the same___ old song. You're__ think - ing you're_gon' do__ me like__ the oth-

- er ones_ be - fore,___ ba - by. Here we go__ a - gain,___ it's the same___ old song. Oh,___ straight-

Play 3 times

- en up__ your act___ or else___ I'm walk - ing out__ the door.__

Repeat ad lib. & fade

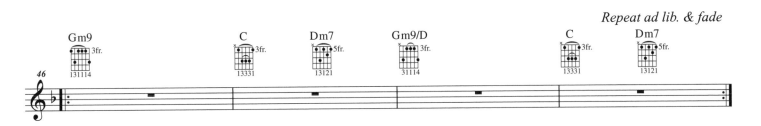

Verse 2:
All this time I thought that I was the one
Who had the problem, oh yeah, mmm.
I gave you everythin', hopin' things might change,
But still you ain't around, so, whoa.
(To Pre-chorus:)

GIRL ON FIRE

Words and Music by
BILLY SQUIER, JEFFREY BHAKSER,
ALICIA KEYS and SALAAM REMI

Girl on Fire - 4 - 4

GIVE UP THE FUNK
(TEAR THE ROOF OFF THE SUCKER)

Words and Music by
GEORGE CLINTON, BOOTSY COLLINS
and JEROME BRAILEY

Moderate funk ♩ = 106

Intro:
N.C.

Tear the roof off, we're gon-na tear the roof off the moth-er, suck-er, tear the roof off the suck-er. Tear the

*E7

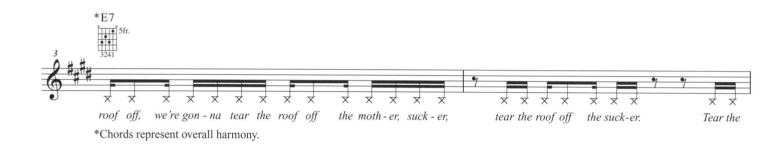

roof off, we're gon-na tear the roof off the moth-er, suck-er, tear the roof off the suck-er. Tear the

*Chords represent overall harmony.

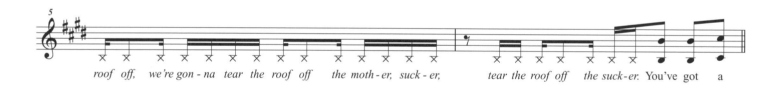

roof off, we're gon-na tear the roof off the moth-er, suck-er, tear the roof off the suck-er. You've got a

Verse:
E7

Elec. Gtr. 1 *(clean-tone)*

real type of thing go-ing down, get-tin' down,_____ there's a

Give Up the Funk (Tear the Roof off the Sucker) - 4 - 1

Chorus:

E13

*First time only.

Give Up the Funk (Tear the Roof off the Sucker) - 4 - 2

we need the funk, we gotta have that funk. Ow,___ we want the funk,

Let us in, we'll tear this moth-er out.

give up the funk. Ow,___ we need the funk, we gotta have that funk. Ow,___

Let us in, we'll tear this moth-er out.

We want the funk, give up the funk. We need the funk, we gotta have that funk.

we gotta have that funk. We want the funk, give up the funk.

We're gon-na turn this moth-er out.___ We're gon-na

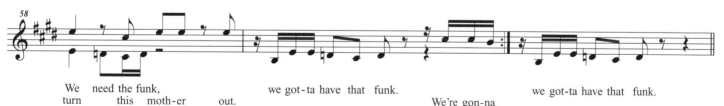

We need the funk, we gotta have that funk. we gotta have that funk.

turn this moth-er out. We're gon-na

Outro:
w/Riffs B & C *(Elec. Gtrs. 1 & 2)*

E7

Repeat ad lib. & fade

We want the funk, give up the funk. We need the funk, we gotta have that funk.

Give Up the Funk (Tear the Roof off the Sucker) - 4 - 4

GOT TO BE REAL

Words and Music by
DAVID PAICH, DAVID FOSTER
and CHERYL LYNN

*Chord names represent overall harmony.

Got to Be Real - 4 - 1

Got to Be Real - 4 - 2

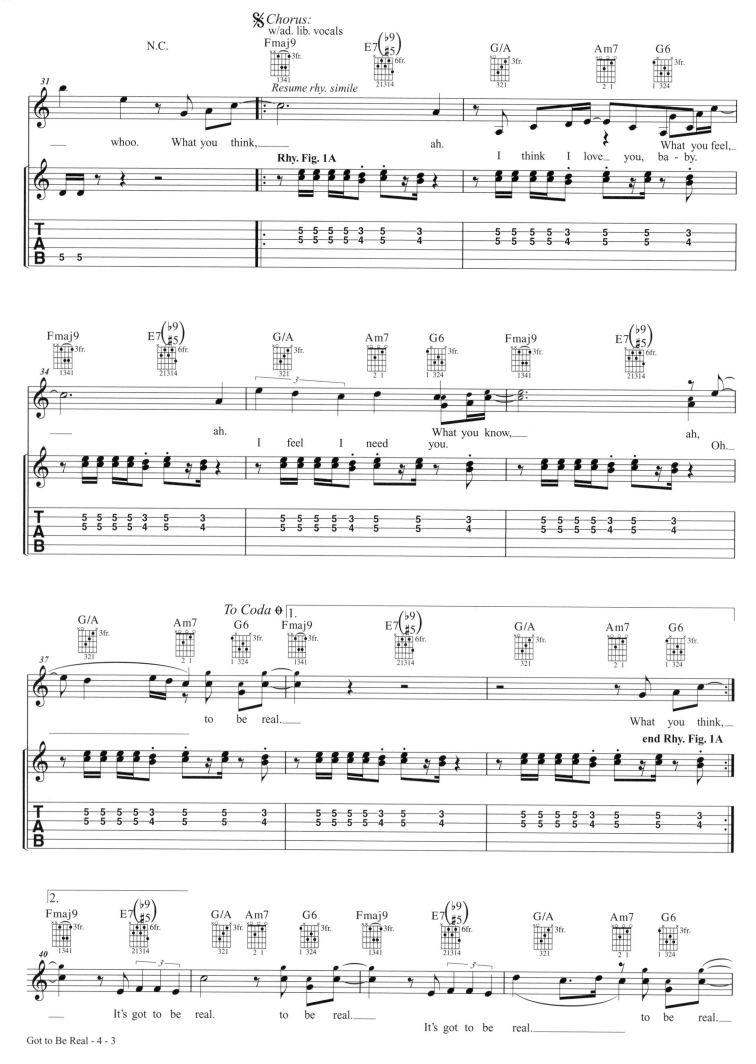

GREATEST LOVE OF ALL

Words by
LINDA CREED

Music by
MICHAEL MASSER

Greatest Love of All - 2 - 1

Greatest Love of All - 2 - 2

HIT THE ROAD JACK

Words and Music by
PERCY MAYFIELD

Hit the Road Jack - 4 - 2

Chorus:

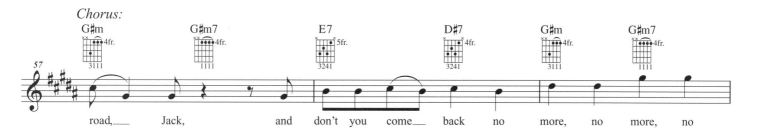

road,___ Jack,　　and don't you come___ back no more, no more, no

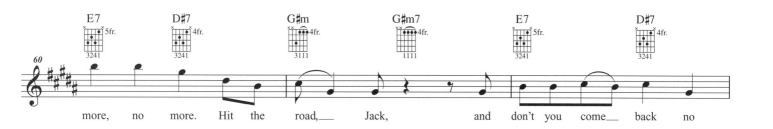

more, no more. Hit the road,___ Jack,　　and don't you come___ back no

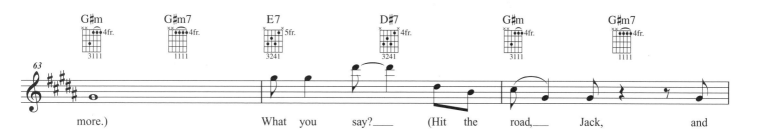

more.)　　　What you say?___ (Hit the road,___ Jack,　and

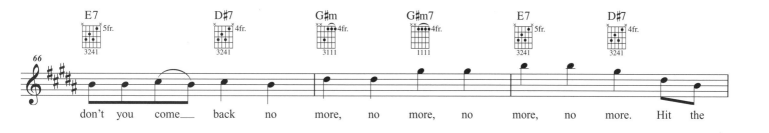

don't you come___ back no more, no more, no more, no more. Hit the

Outro:

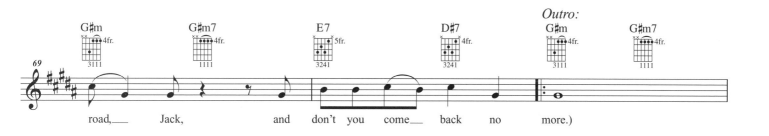

road,___ Jack,　　and don't you come___ back no more.)

Repeat ad lib. and fade

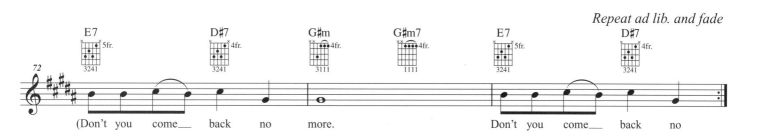

(Don't you come___ back no more.　　Don't you come___ back no

Hit the Road Jack - 4 - 4

HOLD ME, THRILL ME, KISS ME

Words and Music by
HARRY NOBLE

I DON'T HAVE THE HEART

Words and Music by
JUD FRIEDMAN and ALLAN RICH

I Don't Have the Heart - 4 - 1

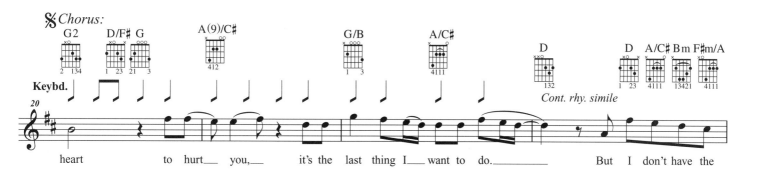

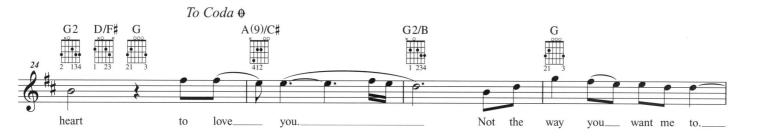

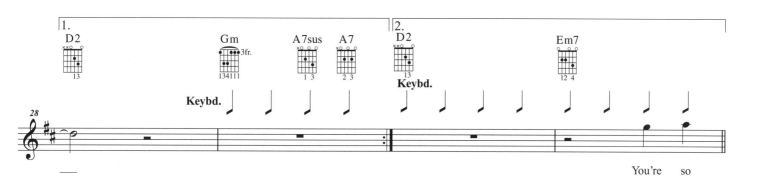

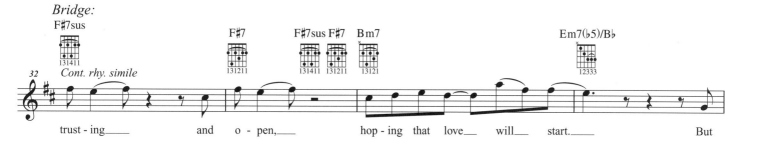

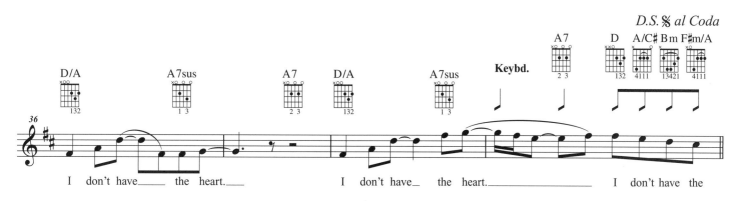

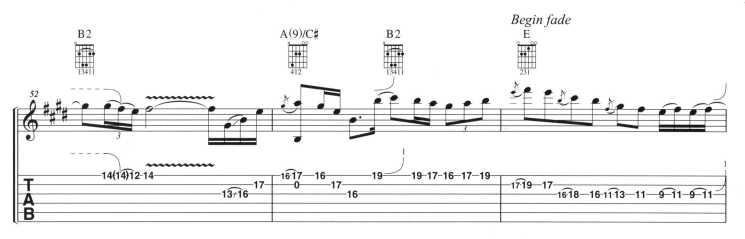

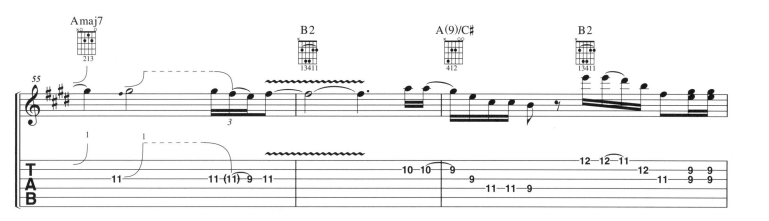

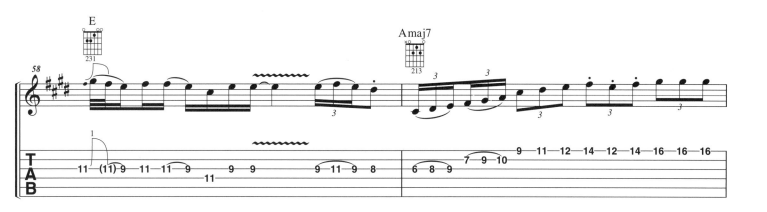

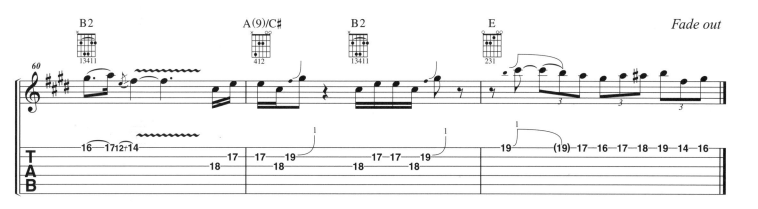

I Don't Have the Heart - 4 - 4

I GOT TO HANDLE IT

Words and Music by
BARNEY BROWNER

I don't know what I'm do-in'. Well, it's time__ I ought__ to say.

I bet-ter get my-self to-geth-er and start work-ing it out__ to-day. I got to

han-dle it, ooh,__ that's what you say.__ I got to han-dle it, ooh,__ if I want your love.__ I got to

han-dle it, mmm,__ ba-by. I got to han-dle it, mmm,__ mmm.__

Interlude:

C7 Bb7 B7

Elec. Gtr.

Horns

Ha, ha, ha!   *Mmm, mmm, mmm, what am I gonna do?*   *Mmm, I tell you this here, I got to…*

w/Backing Vocal Fig., *2 times*

C7

Han-dle it, ba-by, ba-by, ba-by, babe, I got to han-dle it, mmm,__

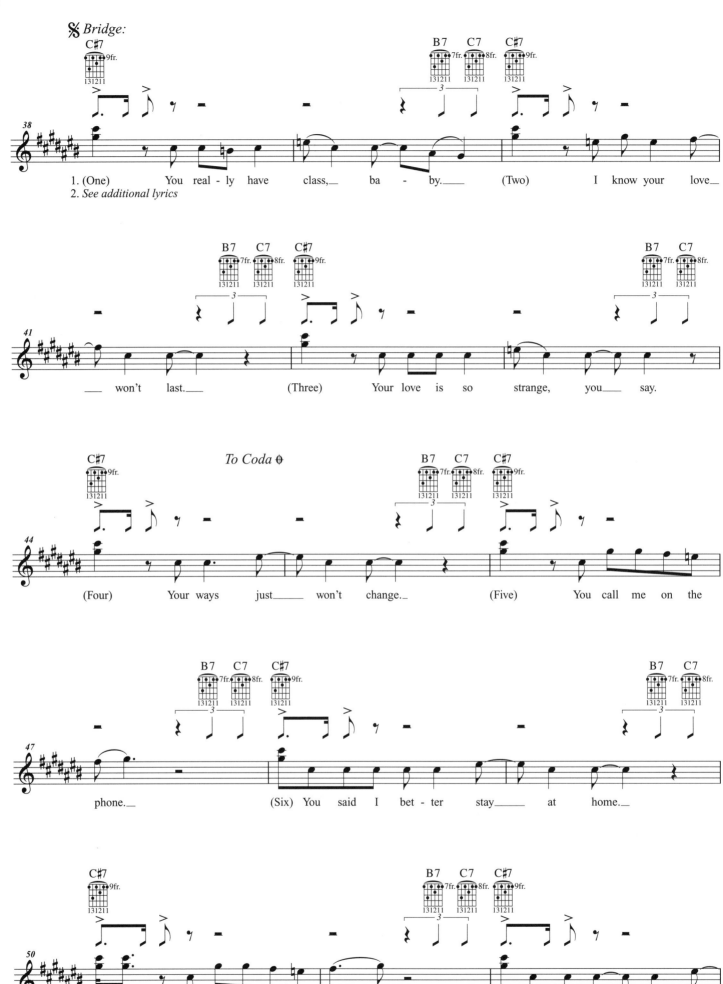

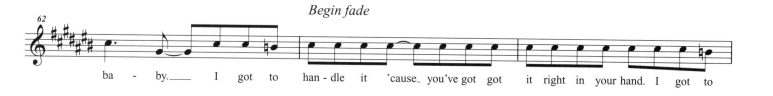

Bridge 2:
(One) The situation is messin' with my reputation.
(Two) Your love for me is miscalculation.
(Three) Every man meets a man's temptation.
(Four) Slow down, this is a new generation.
(To Outro:)

I LIVE FOR YOUR LOVE

Words and Music by
PAM RESWICK, STEVE WERFEL
and RICHARD WAGGONER

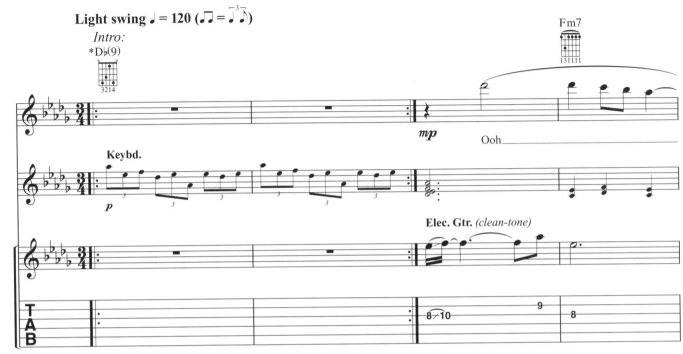

*Chord names represent overall harmony.

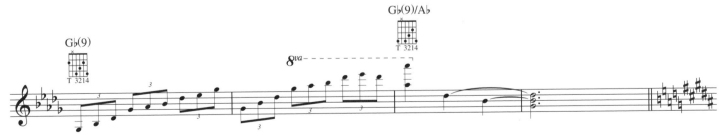

I Live for Your Love - 6 - 1

I Live for Your Love - 6 - 4

I TURN TO YOU

*To match record key, Capo I

Words and Music by
DIANE WARREN

*Recording sounds a half step higher than written.

I Turn to You - 3 - 1

110

NUTBUSH CITY LIMITS

Words and Music by
TINA TURNER

Moderately bright ♩ = 154 (♫ = ♪³♪)

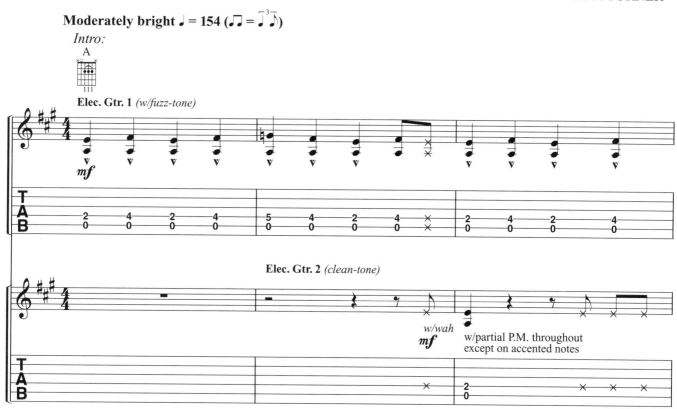

Nutbush City Limits - 5 - 1

112

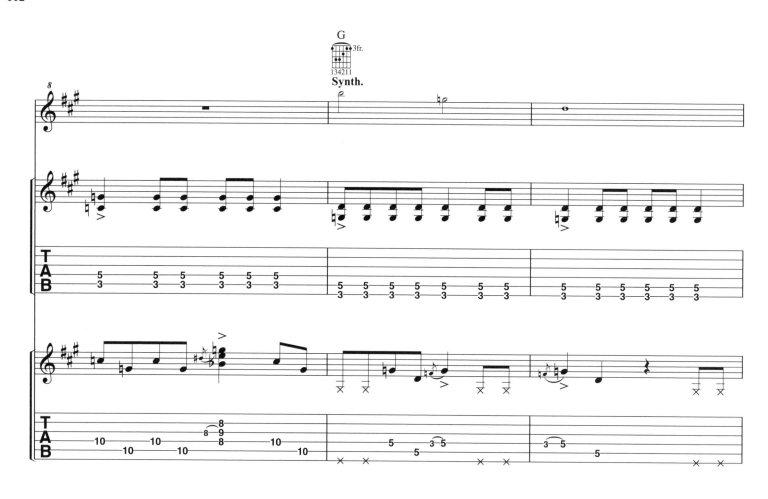

114

Nutbush City Limits - 5 - 4

Verse 3:
You go to fields on weekdays,
And have a picnic on Labor Day.
You go to town on Saturday,
But go to church every Sunday.
They call it Nutbush, oh, Nutbush,
They call it Nutbush city limits.
(To Synth. Solo:)

Verse 4:
No whiskey for sale,
You can't cop no bail.
Salt, pork, and molasses
Is all you get in jail.
They call it Nutbush, oh, Nutbush,
They call it Nutbush city limits.

Outro:
(half-spoken)
Little old town in Tennessee
That's called a quiet little old community.
A one-horse town,
You have to watch what you're puttin' down
In old Nutbush.
They call it Nutbush.

JUST THE WAY YOU ARE (AMAZING)

Words and Music by
KHALIL WALTON, PETER HERNANDEZ,
PHILIP LAWRENCE, ARI LEVINE
and KHARI CAIN

Moderately ♩ = 112

Intro:

Just the Way You Are (Amazing) - 4 - 1

118

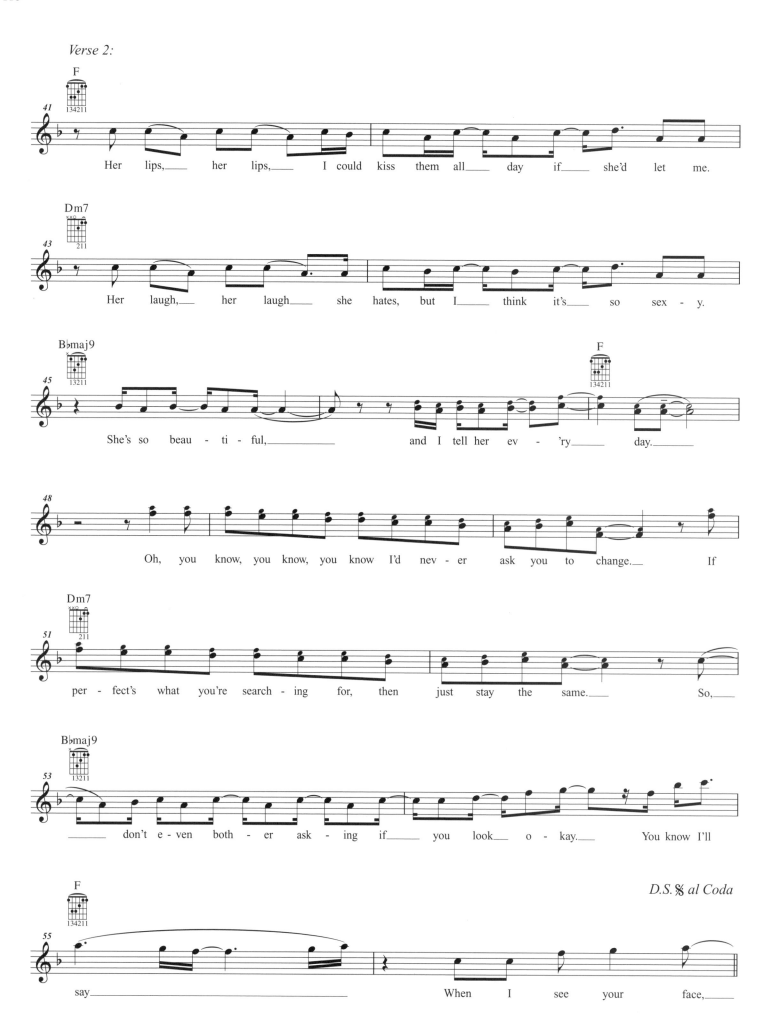

Just the Way You Are (Amazing) - 4 - 3

LADY LOVE ME (ONE MORE TIME)

Words and Music by
JAMES NEWTON HOWARD
and DAVID PAICH

Lady Love Me (One More Time) - 4 - 1

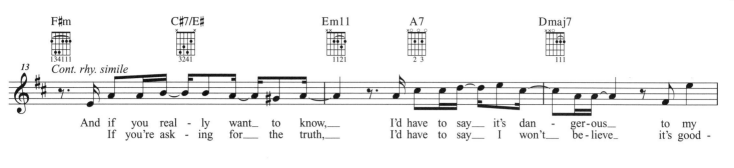

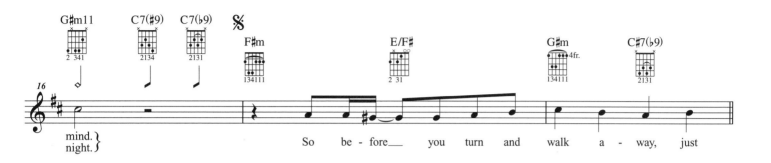

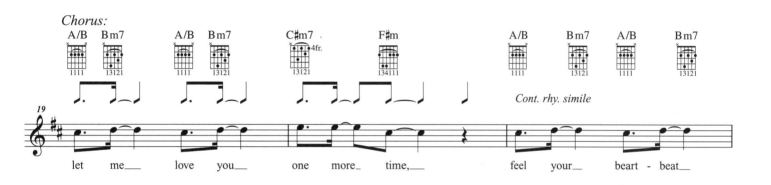

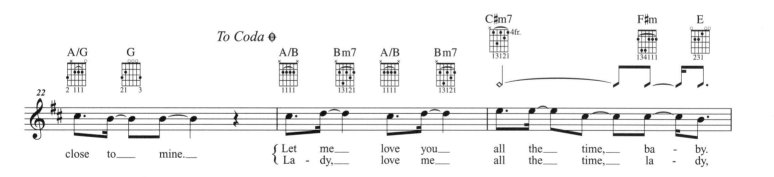

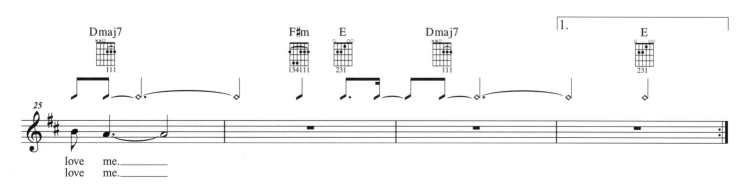

Lady Love Me (One More Time) - 4 - 2

*With scat vocals throughout.

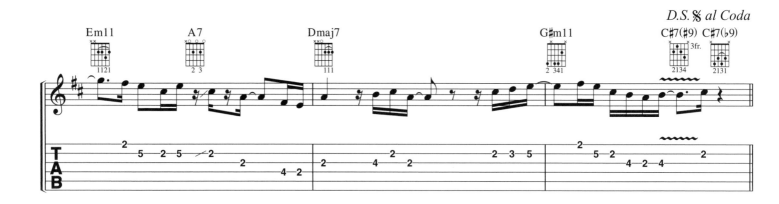

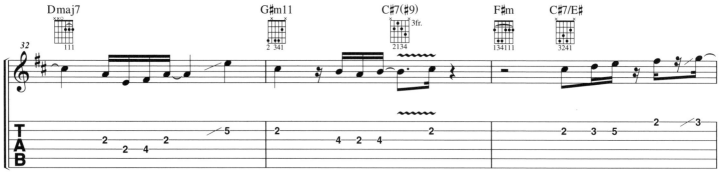

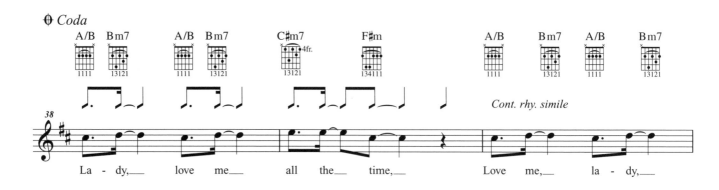

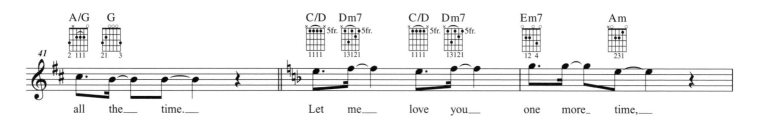

Lady Love Me (One More Time) - 4 - 3

LET'S STAY TOGETHER

Words and Music by
WILLIE MITCHELL, AL GREEN and AL JACKSON

(Whispered:) Let's stay together.

1. I'm,
2.3. *See additional lyrics*

I'm so___ in love with you.___

What-ev-er you want to do is-a all right with

Rhy. Fig. 1

Rhy. Fig. 2

*Bass plays D♭.

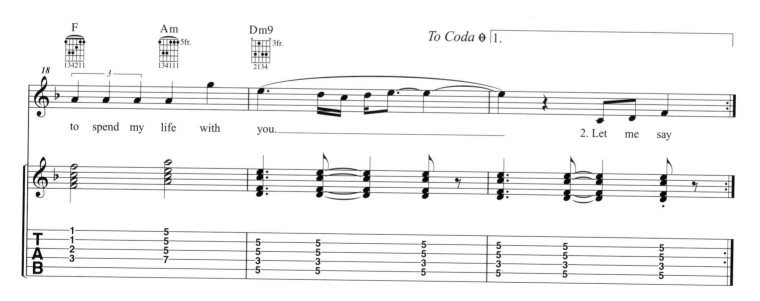

Let's Stay Together - 4 - 2

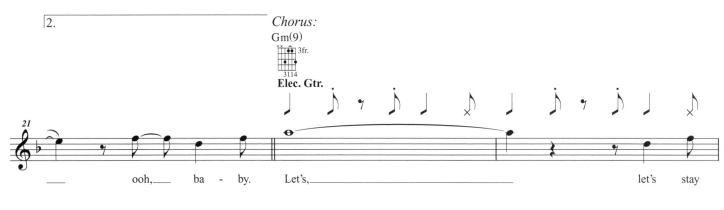

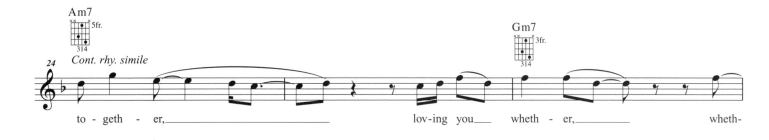

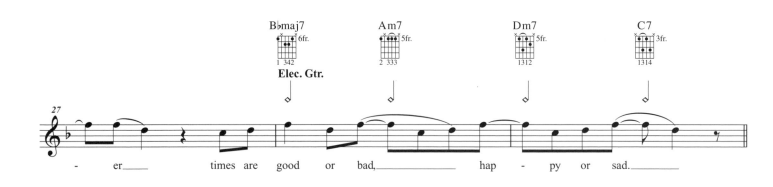

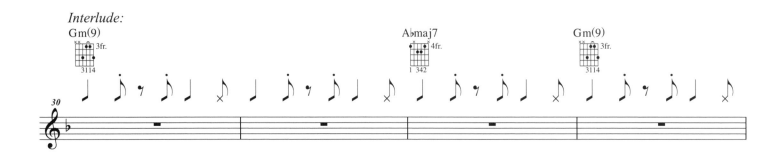

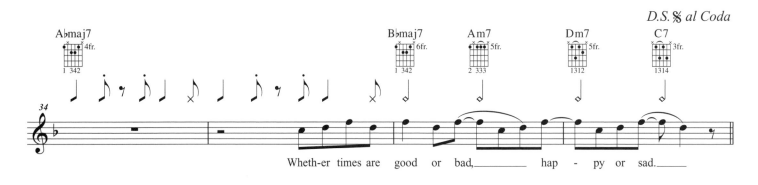

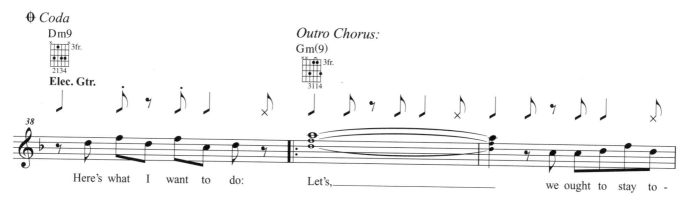

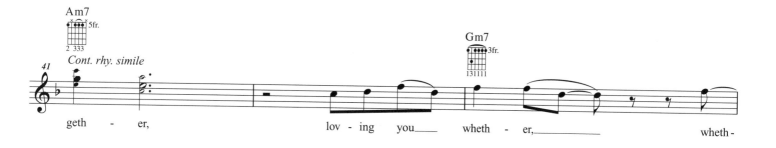

Verse 2:
Let me say since, baby,
Since we've been together, ooo,
Lovin' you forever is what I need.
Let me be the one you come running to
And I'll never be untrue.
(To Chorus:)

Verse 3:
Why, somebody,
Why people break up,
Oh, and turn around a make up?
I just can't see.
You'd never do that to me,
Would you, baby?
Being around you is all I see.
Here's what I want to do:
(To Outro Chorus:)

LIVING IN AMERICA

Words and Music by
DAN HARTMAN and
CHARLIE MIDNIGHT

130

(HEY THERE) LONELY GIRL

Words and Music by
LEON CARR and EARL SHUMAN

(Hey There) Lonely Girl - 4 - 1

(Hey There) Lonely Girl - 4 - 2

136

(Hey There) Lonely Girl - 4 - 3

LOOKIN' FOR A LOVE

*To match record key, Capo V

Words and Music by
J. W. ALEXANDER and ZELDA SAMUELS

*Recording sounds a Perfect Fourth higher than written.

Lookin' for a Love - 2 - 1

Verse 2:
Someone to do a little housework and pamper me again.
(I'm lookin' for a love to call my own.)
Yeah, now with lots of love and kisses and, people, until then.
(I'm lookin' for a love to call my own.)
(To Chorus:)

Verse 3:
Someone in my corner all the way.
(I'm lookin' for a love to call my own.)
She'll be with me to the end, no matter what people say.
(I'm lookin' for a love to call my own.)

Verse 4:
I'll give her my love and soothe her all the time.
(I'm lookin' for a love to call my own.)
I'll be glad to let her know that she's mine all mine.
(I'm lookin' for a love to call my own.)
But, right now…
(To Chorus:)

Lookin' for a Love - 2 - 2

LOWDOWN

Words and Music by
BOZ SCAGGS and DAVID PAICH

*Chords implied by keybd.

1. Ba - by's in - to run - nin' 'round,___ hang - in' with the crowd,___
2.3. See additional lyrics

put - tin' your bus - 'ness in the street,___ talk - in' out loud.___

Say - in' you bought her this and that,___ and how___ much you done spent,

142

Lowdown - 4 - 3

Verse 3:
Nothin' you can't handle,
Nothin' you ain't got,
Put your money on the table
And drive it off the lot.
Turn on that old lovelight
And turn a maybe to a yes,
Same old schoolboy game
Got you into this mess.
Hey, son,
You better get on back to town,
Face the sad old truth,
The dirty lowdown.

(Oooh, oooh,
I wonder, wonder, wonder, wonder who)
Put those ideas in your head.
(Oooh, oooh,
I wonder, wonder, wonder, wonder who.)
(To Interlude:)

Verse 4:
You ain't got to be so bad,
Got to be so cold,
This dog eat dog existence
Sure is gettin' old.
Got to have a Jones for this,
Jones for that,
This runnin' with the Jones's, boy,
Just ain't where it's at.
No, no,
You gonna come back around
To the sad, sad truth,
The dirty lowdown.

(Oooh, oooh,
I wonder, wonder, wonder, wonder who)
Got you thinkin' like that, boy.
(Oooh, oooh,
I wonder, wonder, wonder, wonder who.)
(To Interlude:)

MAMA SAID

Words and Music by
WILLIE DENSON and LUTHER DIXON

Interlude 2:
And then she said someone will look at me
Like I'm looking at you one day,
Then I might find
I don't want you any old way,
So I don't worry 'cause…
(To Coda)

Mama Said - 4 - 4

MOTHER-IN-LAW

Words and Music by
ALLEN TOUSSAINT

149

Mother-in-Law - 2 - 2

MUSTANG SALLY

Words and Music by
BONNY RICE

Mustang Sally - 4 - 1

Begin fade (2nd time)

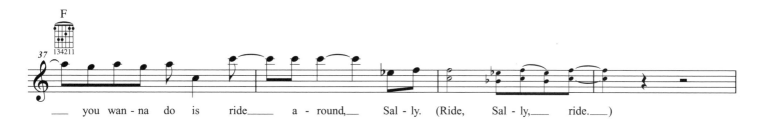

All you wan-na do is ride___ a-round, Sal-ly._____ (Ride, Sal-ly,__ ride.__) All_

__ you wan-na do is ride___ a-round,_ Sal-ly. (Ride, Sal-ly,__ ride.__)

All you wan-na do is__ ride__ a-round, Sal-ly. (Ride, Sal-ly,__ ride.__)

One of these ear-ly morn-ings, yeah,_____ wow, gon-na be wip-in' your weep-in' eyes._

D.S. 𝄋 and fade on Chorus

_____ Huh, What I__ say now._ Look-a here. 2. I

Verse 2:
 I bought you a brand-new Mustang,
A nineteen sixty-five, huh.
Now you come around, signifyin' a woman,
And don't wanna let me ride.
Mustang Sally, now, baby, oh lord,
Guess you'd better slow that Mustang down.
Huh, oh lord, look-a here.
You've been runnin' all over town,
Wow, I got to put your flat feet on the ground.
Huh, what I say now.
Let me say it one more time, y'all,...
(To Chorus:)

Mustang Sally - 4 - 4

OH HAPPY DAY

Moderately ♩ = 114

Words and Music by
EDWIN R. HAWKINS

SOUL TWIST

Moderate swing ♩ = 125 (♫ = ♩♪)

Music by
KING CURTIS

Elec. Gtr. *(w/light overdrive)* **Rhy. Fig. 1**

Soul Twist - 3 - 1

Soul Twist - 3 - 3

OOH CHILD

Words and Music by
STAN VINCENT

Ooh Child - 4 - 1

162

Ooh Child - 4 - 4

PICK UP THE PIECES

By ROGER BALL, MALCOLM DUNCAN, ALAN GORRIE,
HAMISH STUART, ROBBIE McINTOSH, and OWEN McINTYRE

*On original recording, rhythm guitar plays strings 1–3 only.

*On original recording, rhythm guitar plays strings 1–3 only.

To Coda ⊕

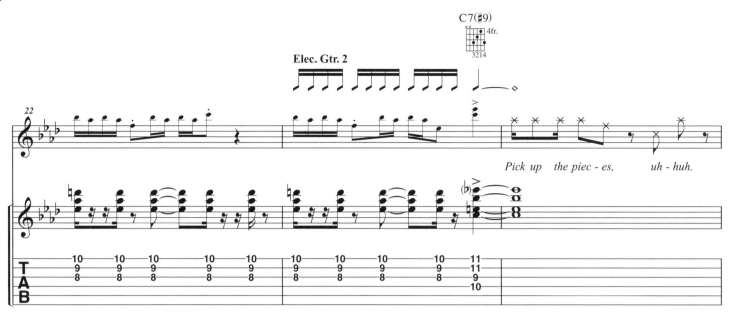

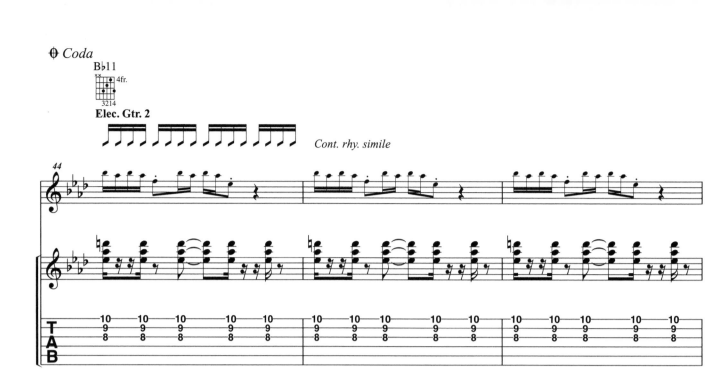

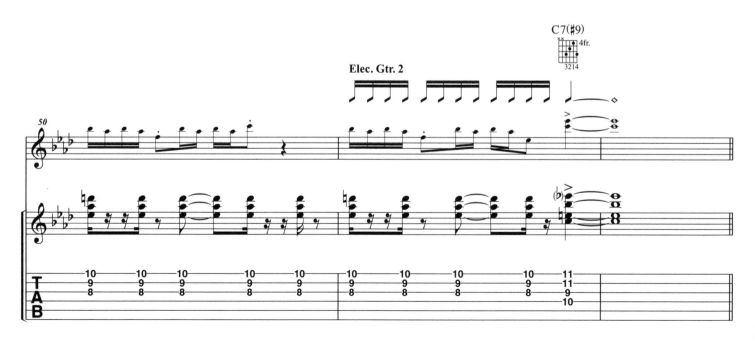

PLAY THAT FUNKY MUSIC

Words and Music by
ROBERT PARISSI

Play That Funky Music - 6 - 1

SHAKE A TAIL FEATHER

Words and Music by
OTHA HAYES, VERLIE RICE
and ANDRE WILLIAMS

Shake a Tail Feather - 4 - 1

Shake a Tail Feather - 4 - 2

SUAVECITO

Words and Music by
RICHARD BEAN
*Arranged by RICHARD BEAN,
PABLO TELLEZ and ABEL ZARATE*

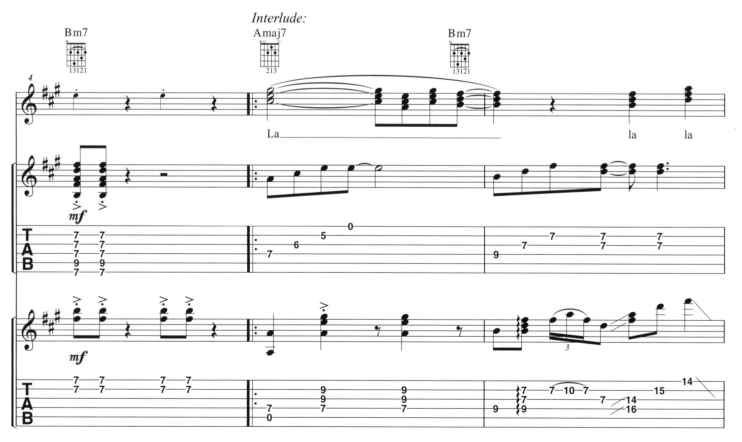

*Chord frames reflect implied harmony throughout.

Suavecito - 6 - 1

Suavecito - 6 - 2

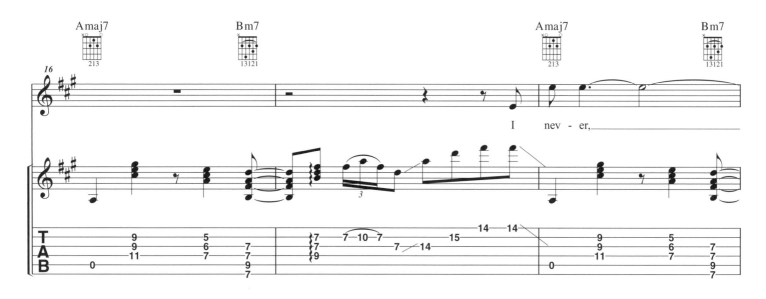

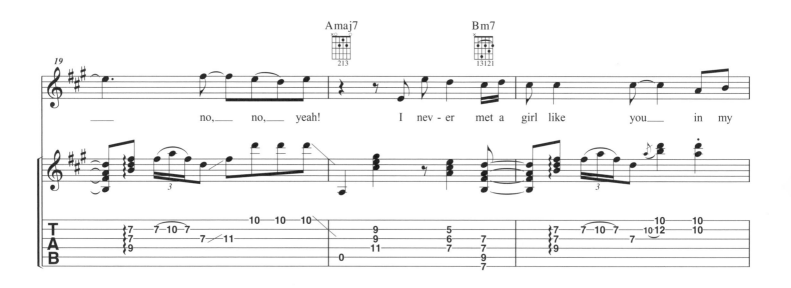

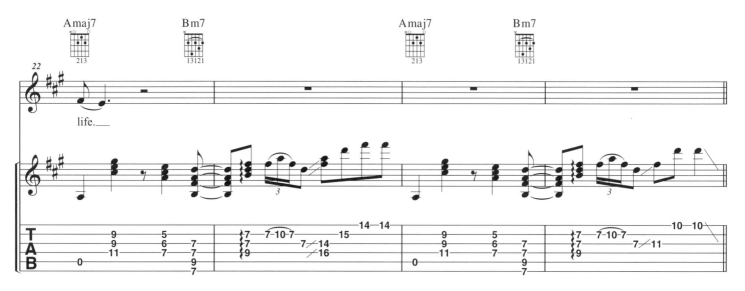

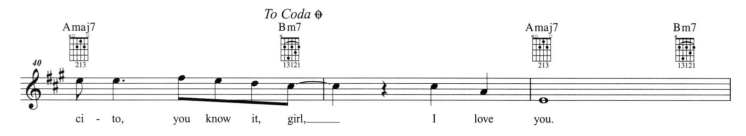

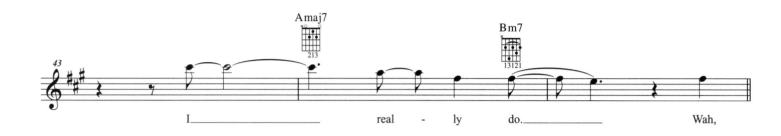

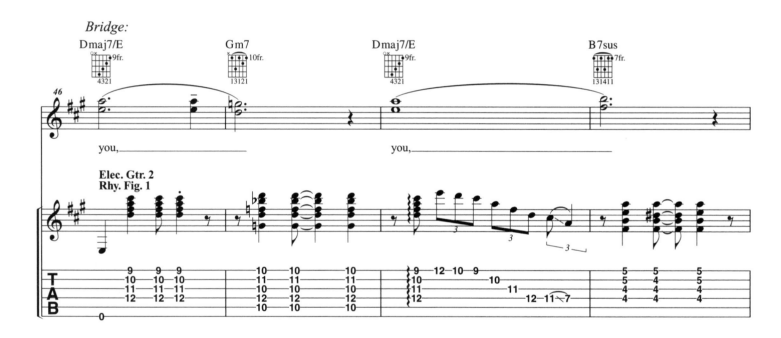

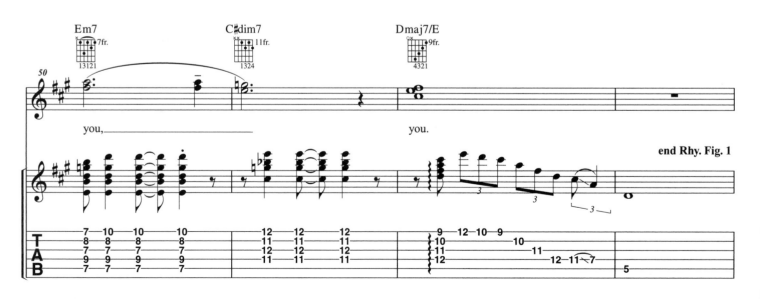

SWEET SOUL MUSIC

Words and Music by
SAM COOKE
Additional Material by
ARTHUR CONLEY and OTIS REDDING

THAT'S HOW IT FEELS

Words and Music by
BOBBY WOMACK and DON COVAY

That's How It Feels - 5 - 1

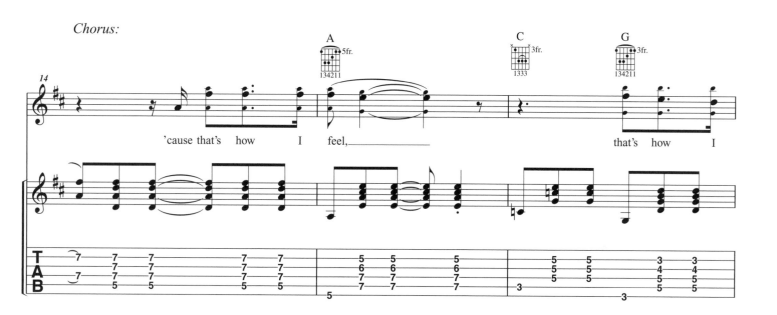

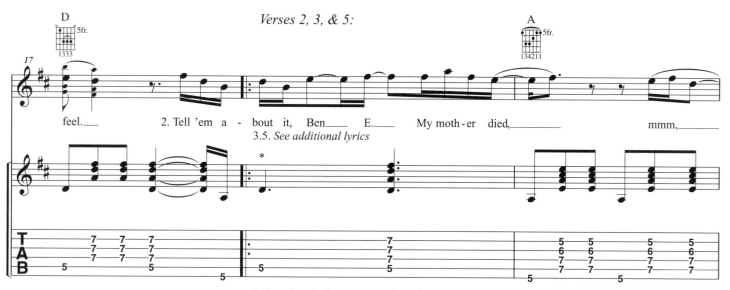

*Elec. Gtr. simile on repeats throughout.

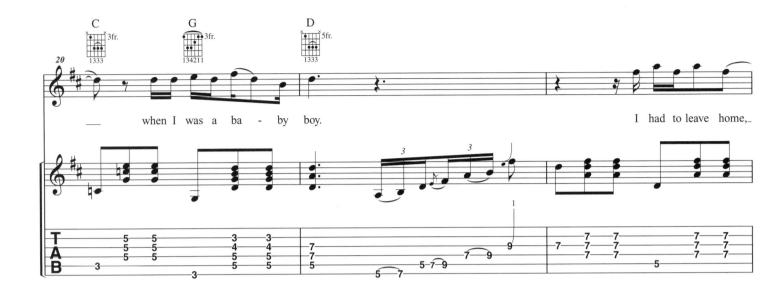

when I was a ba - by boy.

I had to leave home,

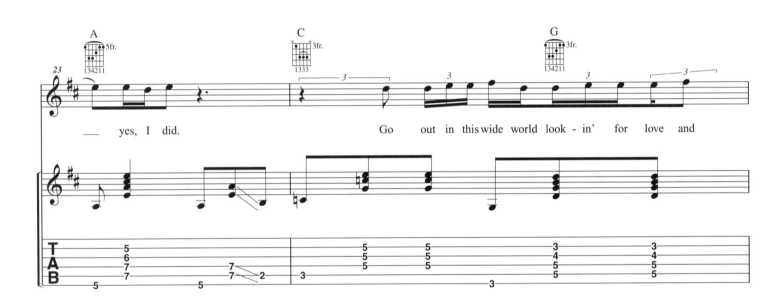

yes, I did.

Go out in this wide world look - in' for love and

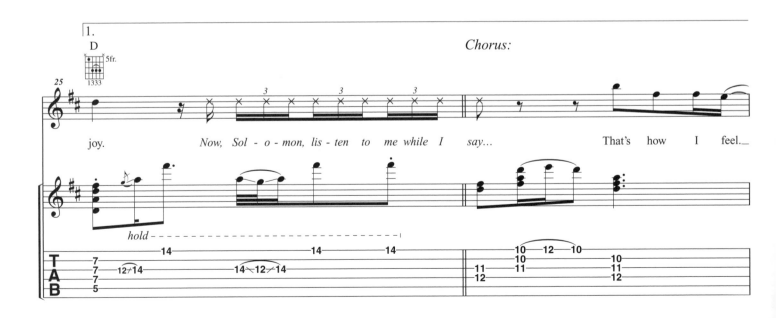

joy.

Now, Sol - o - mon, lis - ten to me while I say...

That's how I feel.

Verse 3:
Listen to me, huh!
You see, some folks are often blamed and accused,
Usually for things that they don't do.
But, you see, I know that everybody needs somebody.
And I'm so grateful, baby, that I've got you.
(To Bridge:)

Verse 4:
Solomon, let me tell you something; a true story...
I got one sister, Lord, and eight of us boys.
I was thirteen-years-old, yeah, oh yeah,
Before I got my first Christmas toy.
And let me tell you this...
(To Chorus:)

Verse 5:
Don, listen to me.
Tell 'em about it, Joe Tex.
I remember the first day, I was six-years-old, y'all.
Mama took me into school.
Listen to me. Things was so tough back then, y'all,
I had to wear my daddy's old brokedown shoes.
Ha ha! Listen...
(To Coda)

That's How It Feels - 5 - 5

TREAT HER LIKE A LADY

Words and Music by
EDDIE CORNELIUS

Treat Her Like a Lady - 3 - 1

Verse 2:
I know you've heard that a woman
Will soon take advantage of you.
Let me tell you, my friend,
There just ain't no substitute.

Chorus 2:
You ought to treat her like a lady.
Oh, the best you can do.
You got to treat her like a lady, she'll give in to you.
Now, hook and sinker, you know what I mean.
(To Bridge:)

Verse 3:
So, my friends, now there you have it,
I said it's easy simple way.
If you fail to do this,
Don't blame her if she looks me way.

Chorus 3:
'Cause I'm gonna treat her like a lady,
So affectionately.
I'm gonna treat her like a lady, she'll give in to me.
Now, hook and sinker, you know what I mean.
(To Outro Chorus:)

THIS MASQUERADE

Words and Music by
LEON RUSSELL

Moderately ♩ = 96

Intro:

Elec. Gtr. 1

Cont. rhy. simile

Elec. Gtr. 2

*Elec. Gtr. 2 dbld. by scat vocal.

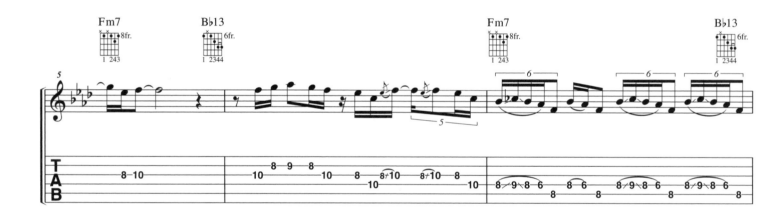

This Masquerade - 4 - 1

*Elec. Gtr. 2 dbld. by scat vocal.

This Masquerade - 4 - 4

TOO LATE TO TURN BACK NOW

Words and Music by
EDDIE CORNELIUS

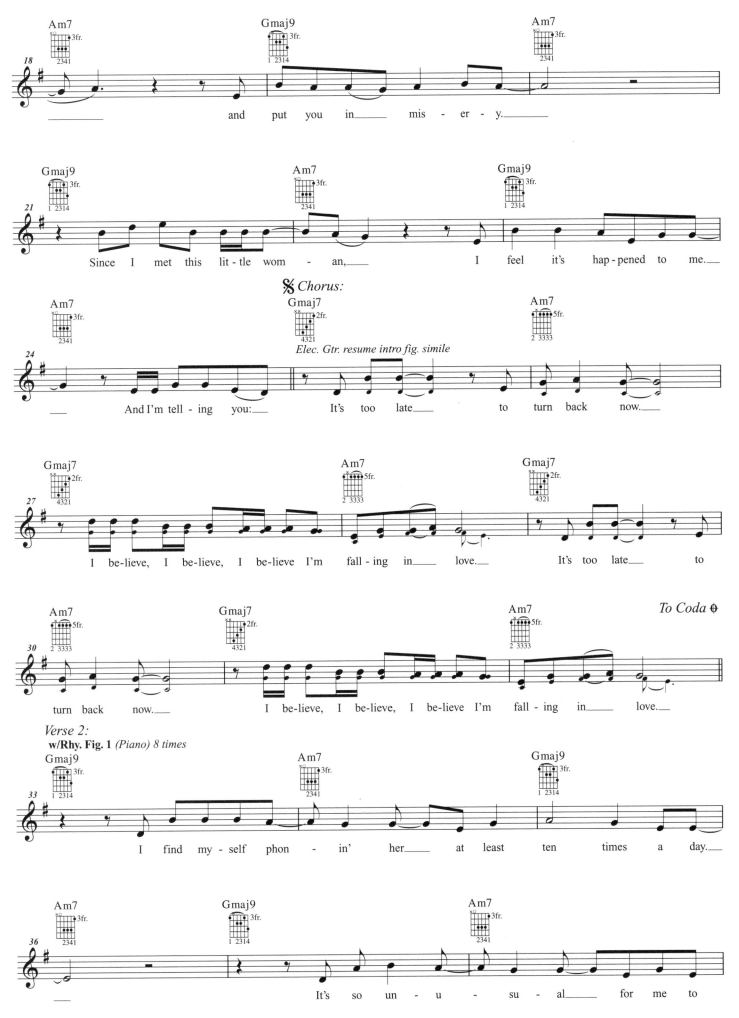

Too Late to Turn Back Now - 4 - 2

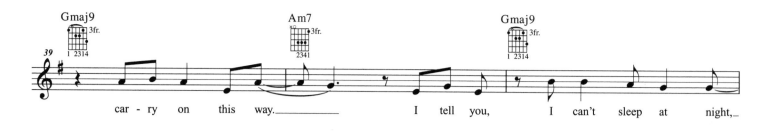

carry on this way.＿　I tell you, I can't sleep at night,＿

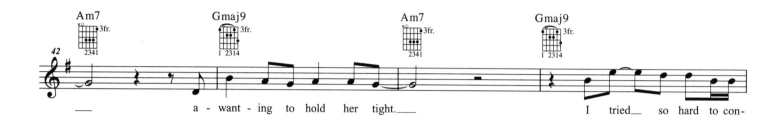

＿ a-want-ing to hold her tight.＿　I tried＿ so hard to con-

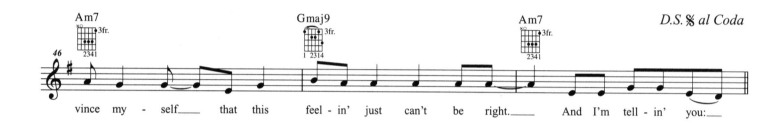

vince my-self＿ that this feel-in' just can't be right.＿　And I'm tell-in' you:＿

D.S. ％ al Coda

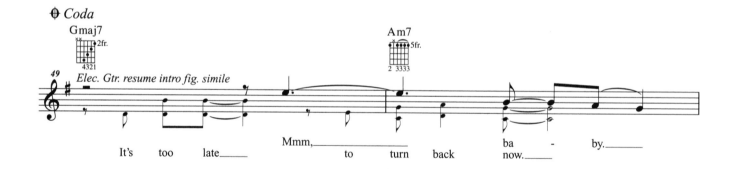

✛ *Coda*

Elec. Gtr. resume intro fig. simile

It's too late＿　Mmm,＿＿ to turn back now.＿ ba - by.＿

I be-lieve, I be-lieve, I be-lieve I'm fall-ing in＿ love.＿　It's too late,＿ ba -
All＿＿＿＿＿＿＿＿　right.＿　It's too late＿ to

-　by.＿ now.　I tell you.　I be-lieve, I be-lieve, I be-lieve I'm fall-ing in＿ love.＿
turn back now.＿　　　　Oh.＿＿＿＿

Too Late to Turn Back Now - 4 - 3

TOSSIN' AND TURNIN'

Words and Music by
MALOU RENE and RITCHIE ADAMS

Tossin' and Turnin' - 4 - 1

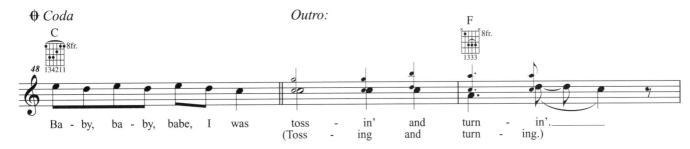

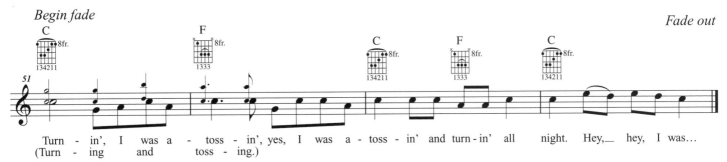

Verse 2:
I kicked the blankets on the floor,
Turned my pillow upside down.
I never, never did before
Because I was tossin' and turnin'.
Turnin' and tossin'.
A-tossin' and turnin' all night.
(To Bridge:)

Verse 3:
The clock downstairs was strikin' four,
Couldn't get you off my mind.
I heard the milkman at the door,
'Cause I was tossin' and turnin'.
Turnin' and tossin'.
A-tossin' and turnin' all night.
(To Sax Solo:)

Verse 4:
The clock downstairs was strikin' four,
I couldn't get you off my mind.
I heard the milkman at the door,
'Cause I was tossin' and turnin'.
Turnin' and tossin'.
A-tossin' and turnin' …
(To Outro:)

Tossin' and Turnin' - 4 - 4

TRY A LITTLE TENDERNESS

Words and Music by
HARRY WOODS, JIMMY CAMPBELL
and REG CONNELLY

Slowly and freely

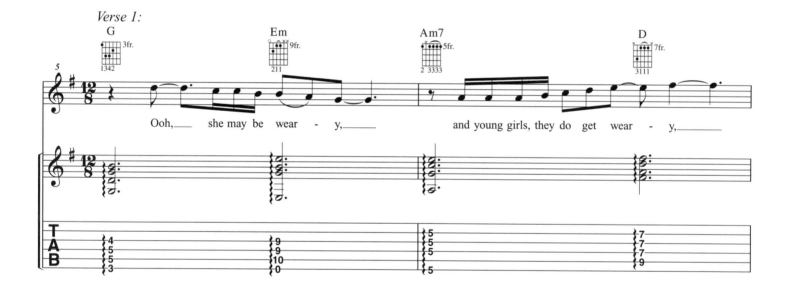

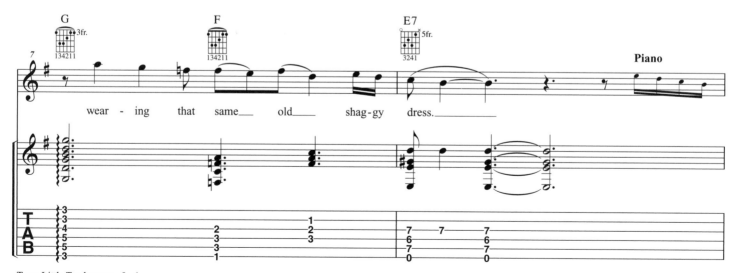

Try a Little Tenderness - 5 - 1

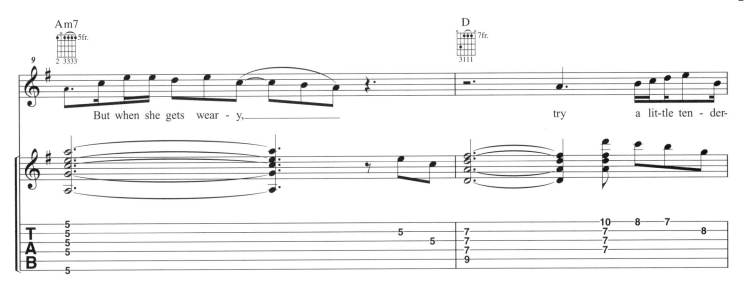

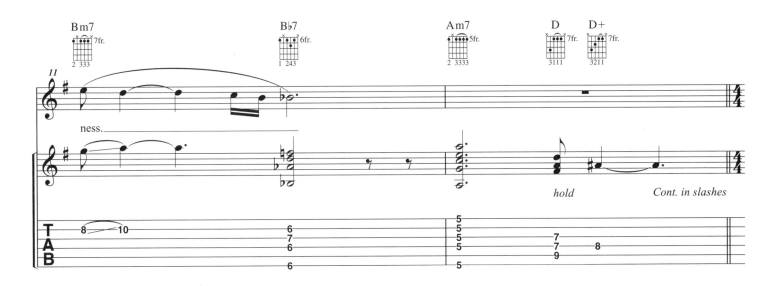

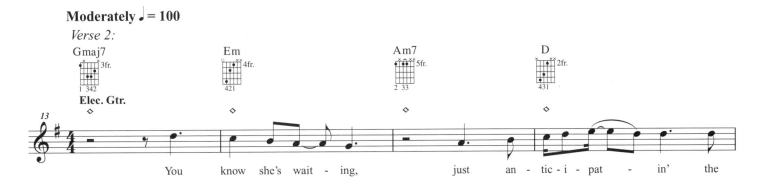

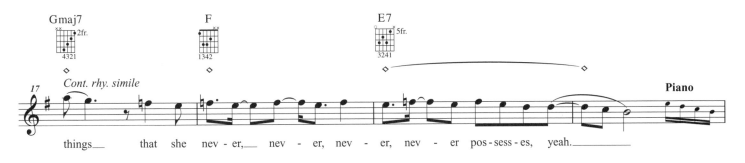

Try a Little Tenderness - 5 - 2

212

so eas - y,_____ all you got-ta do is try, try a lit - tle

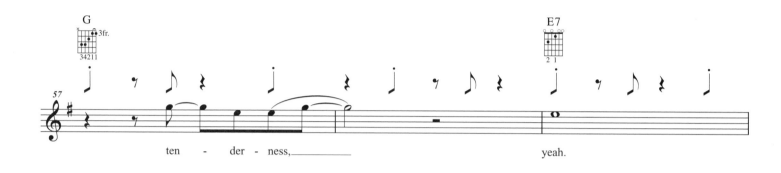

ten - der - ness,_____ yeah.

Outro:

Squeeze her, tease her, nev-er leave her, you got to, you

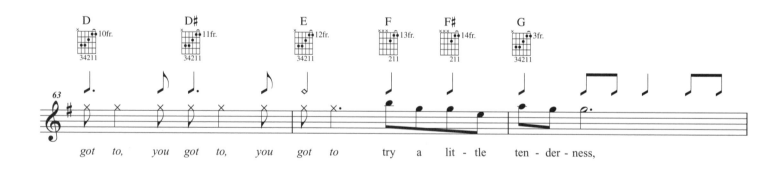

got to, you got to, you got to try a lit - tle ten - der - ness,

Repeat ad lib. & fade

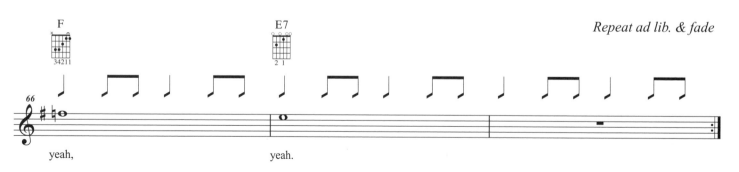

yeah, yeah.

UN-BREAK MY HEART

Words and Music by
DIANE WARREN

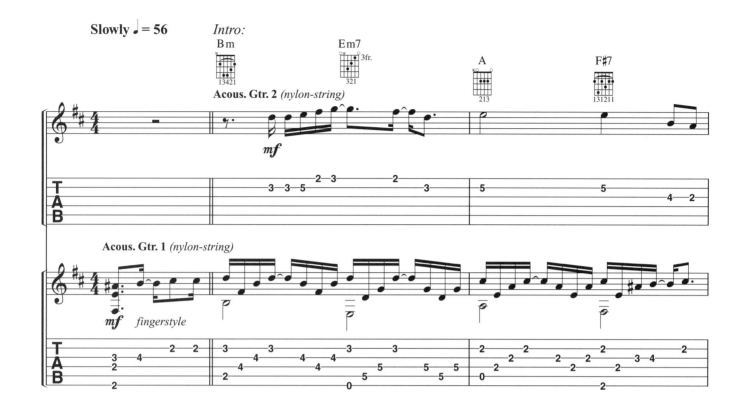

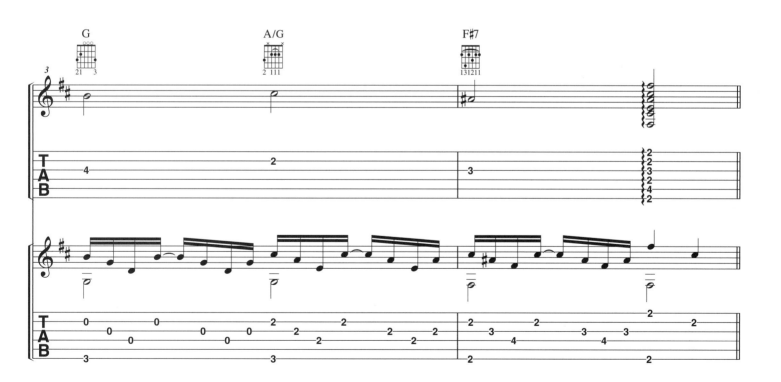

Un-Break My Heart - 5 - 1

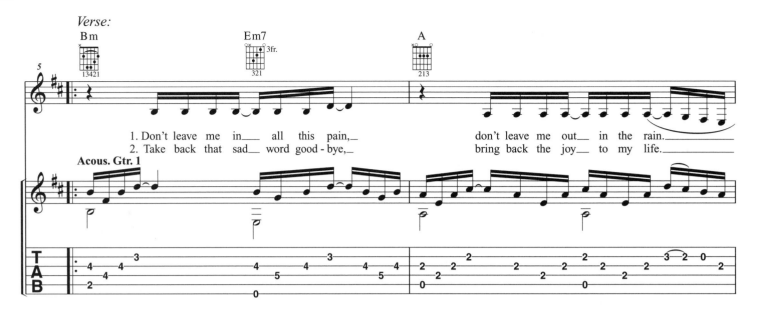

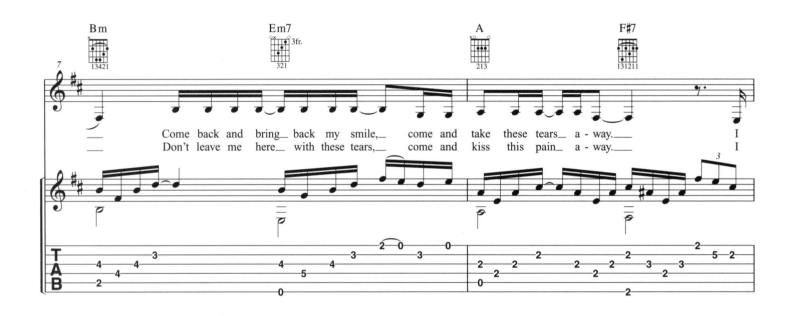

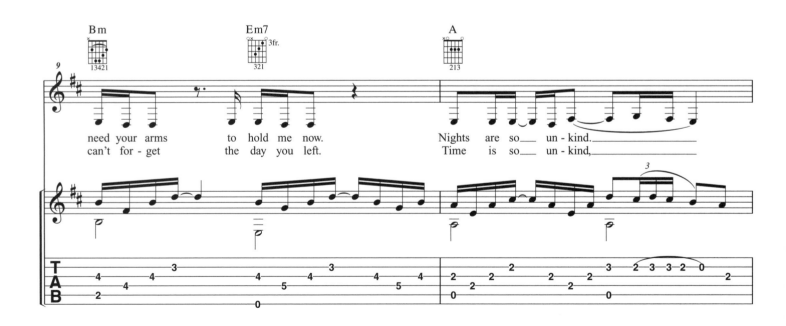

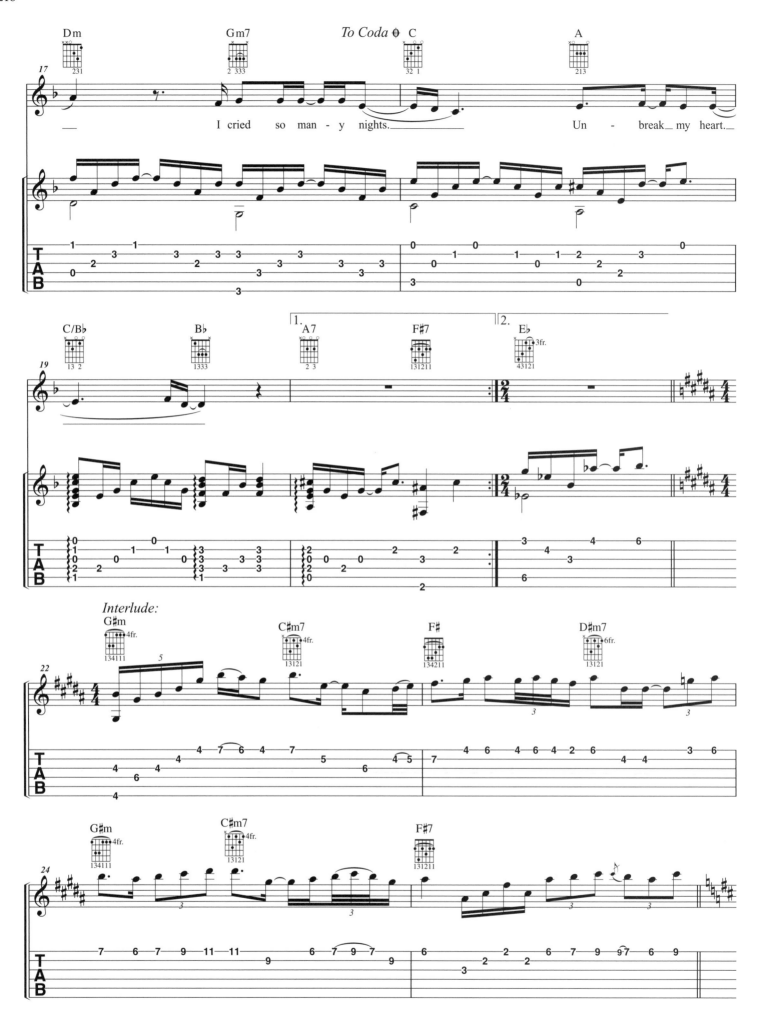

UNCHAIN MY HEART

*To match recording, tune down 1/2 step:

⑥ = E♭ ③ = G♭
⑤ = A♭ ② = B♭
④ = D♭ ① = E♭

Words and Music by
BOBBY SHARP and TEDDY POWELL

Latin, moderately fast ♩ = 152

Intro:
Am

Un-chain my heart,

Horns *(arr. for gtr.)*   **Riff A**   **end Riff A**

mf

*Recording sounds a half step lower than written.

Verse 1:
Am6

Piano

mf   *Cont. rhy. simile*

(Un - chain my heart.)   ba - by, let me be.   (Un - chain my heart.)   Un - chain my heart,

F13   Am6

(Un - chain my heart.)   'cause you don't care a - bout me.   (Un - chain my heart.)

Dm6   Am6   Dm6   Am6

You've got me sewn up like a pil - low - case,   but you let my love go to waste. So, un - chain
(Ahh.   )   (Ahh.   )

F7   E7   **w/Riff A** *(Horns)*
Am

my heart, oh please, please set me free.   Un - chain my heart,
(Ahh.   )

© 1961 (Renewed) B. SHARP MUSIC
Print Rights for the U.S. and all Rights for Canada Administered by MUSIC SALES CORPORATION
All Rights Reserved   Used by Permission

Unchain My Heart - 4 - 1

Unchain My Heart - 4 - 4

WATCH YOUR STEP

Words and Music by
BOBBY PARKER

Begin fade

thing you do.__ I'm gon - na keep my eyes a - fo - cused
(Watch your step.) (Watch your step.)

Fade out

right on__ you.__ You're gon - na look out run - nin' ev - 'ry where you go.
(Watch your step.) (Watch your step.)

Verse 3:
I'm gonna miss your money every night.
When I get myself together,
Gonna be all right, now.
(Watch your step, watch your step,
Watch your step, watch your step.)
Move me by your side and
I'm gonna say go somewhere and hide.
Hey.
(To Chorus:)

THE WAH-WATUSI

Words and Music by
KAL MANN and DAVID APPELL

The Wah-Watusi - 3 - 1

Bridge:

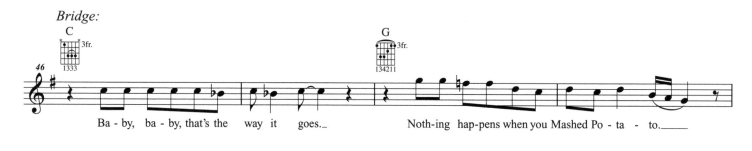

Ba - by, ba - by, that's the way it goes.___ Noth-ing hap-pens when you Mashed Po - ta - to.___

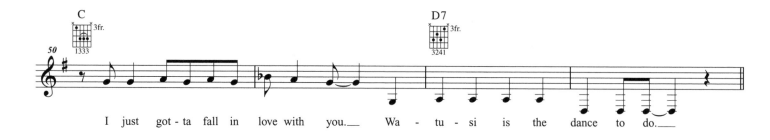

I just got - ta fall in love with you.___ Wa - tu - si is the dance to do.___

Outro:

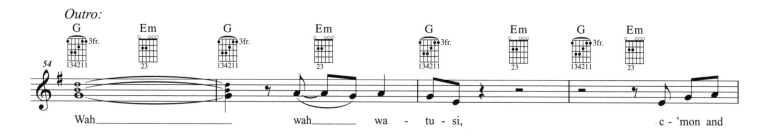

Wah___ wah___ wa - tu - si, c - 'mon and

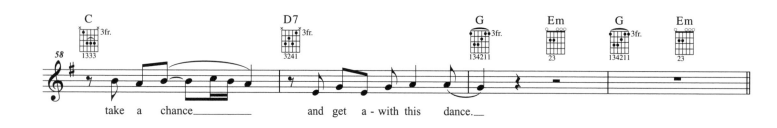

take a chance___ and get a - with this dance.___

Begin fade

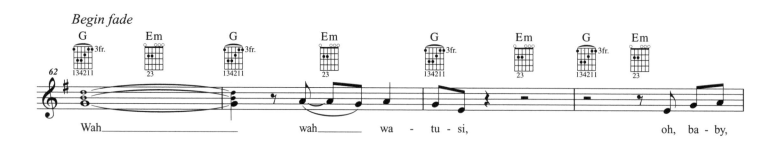

Wah___ wah___ wa - tu - si, oh, ba - by,

Fade out

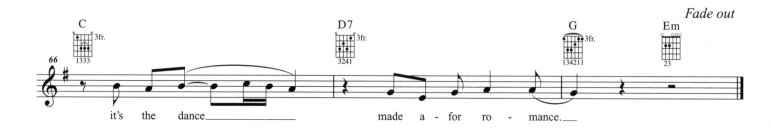

it's the dance___ made a - for ro - mance.___

The Wah-Watusi - 3 - 3

(WHAT A) WONDERFUL WORLD

Words and Music by
SAM COOKE, HERB ALPERT and LOU ADLER

(What a) Wonderful World - 3 - 1

234

Don't know much a - bout the French I took.___ But I do know that
Don't know what a slide___ rule is for.___ But I do know one and

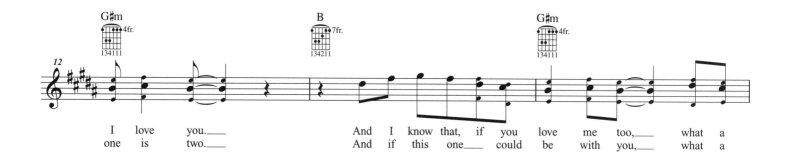

I love you.___ And I know that, if you love me too,___ what a
one is two.___ And if this one___ could be with you,___ what a

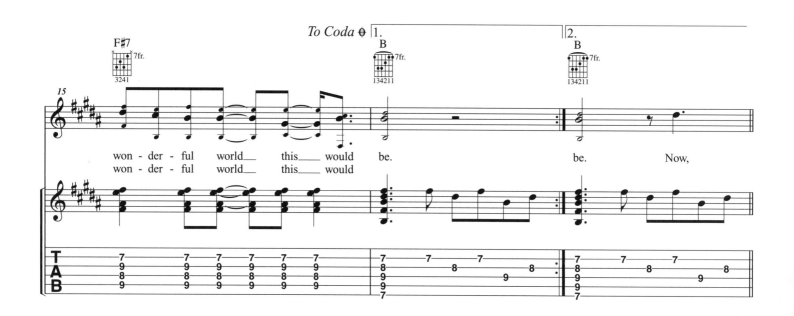

wonderful world___ this___ would be.   be.   Now,
wonderful world___ this___ would be.

Bridge:

I don't claim___ to be an A stu-dent,___ but I'm try'n' to be. For,

YES, I'M READY

Words and Music by
BARBARA MASON

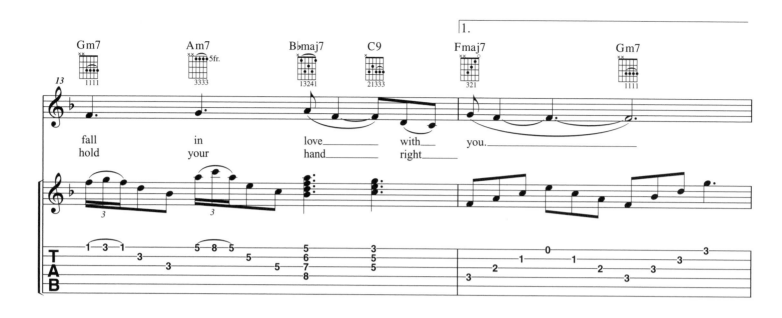

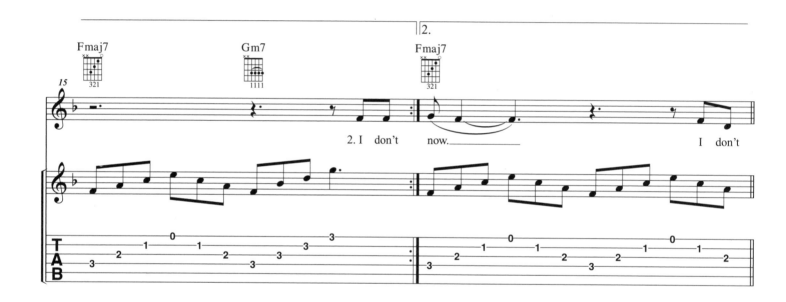

YOU BETTER MOVE ON

*Recording sounds slightly sharp.

Words and Music by
ARTHUR ALEXANDER

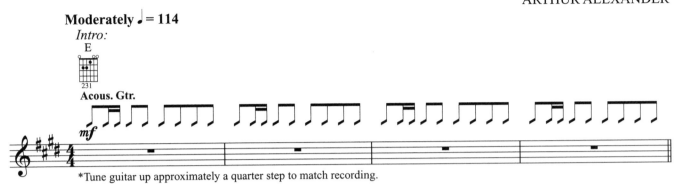

*Tune guitar up approximately a quarter step to match recording.

*Elec. Gtr. enters on repeat.

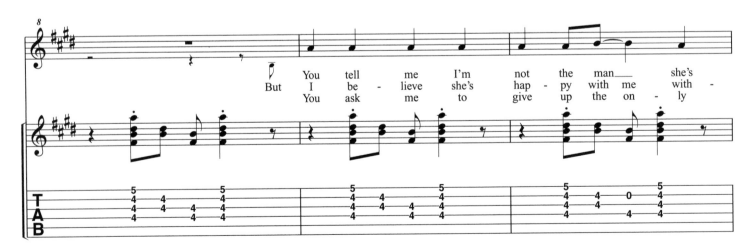

You Better Move On - 4 - 1

Bridge:

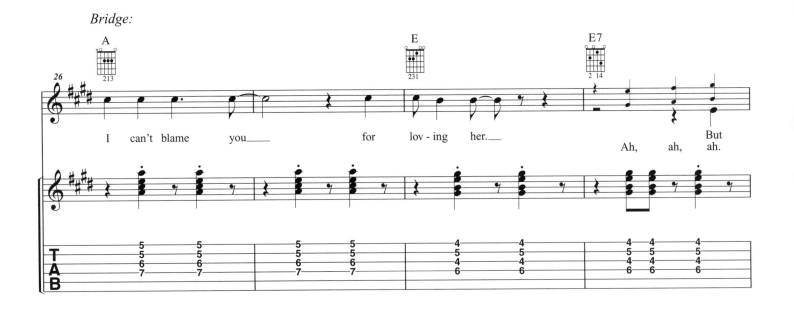

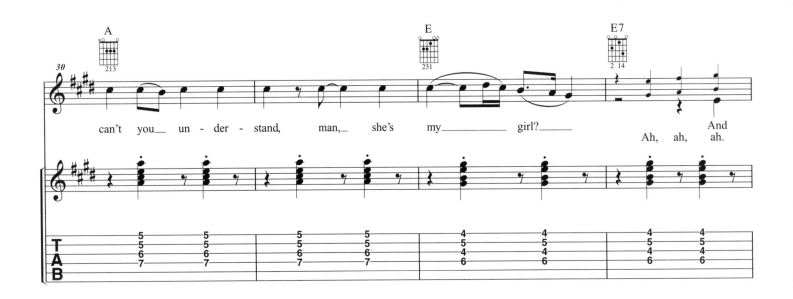

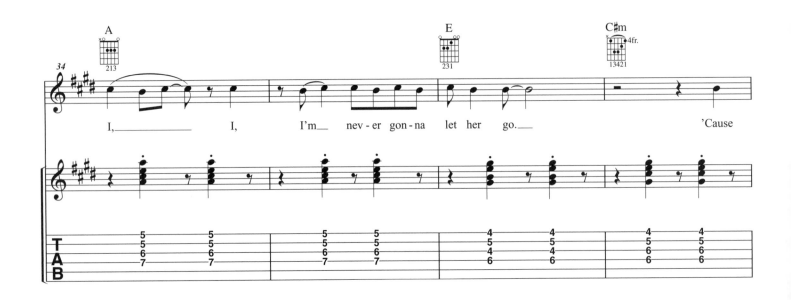

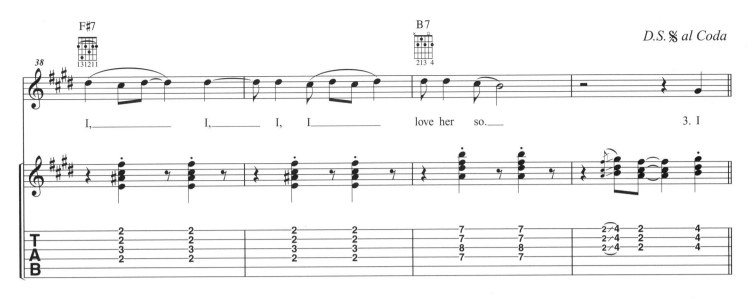

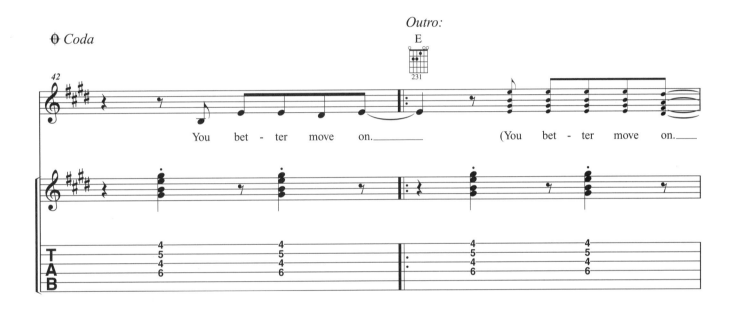

YOU SEND ME

Words and Music by
SAM COOKE

You Send Me - 4 - 1

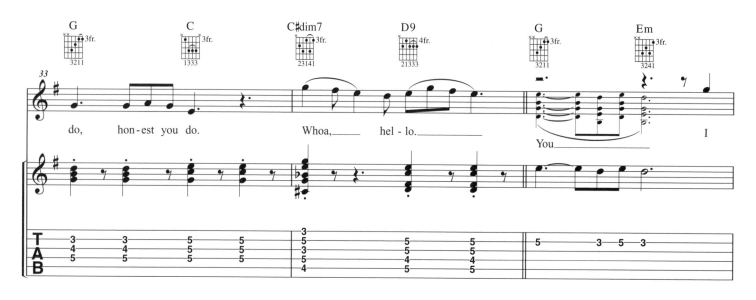

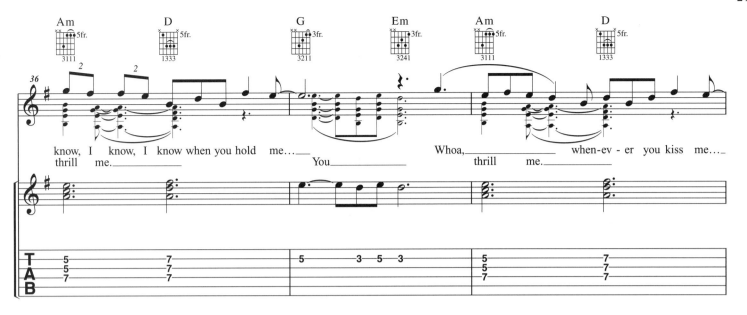

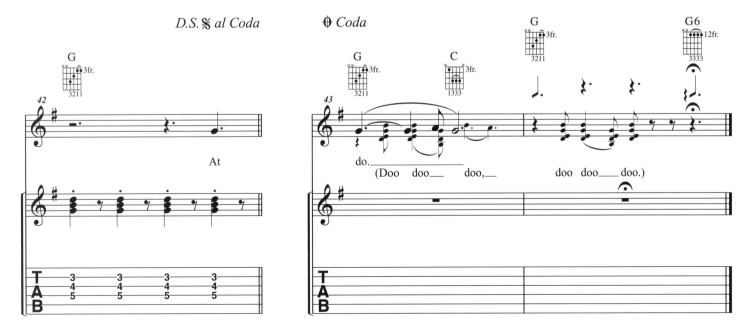

You Send Me - 4 - 4

YOU BETTER KNOW IT

Words and Music by
JACKIE WILSON

Well,_ I want you to run to me, ba - by, a run with all your might._ I wan - na love you, pret - ty ba - by, 'til the broad day - light. Wan - na fill you,_ pret - ty ma - ma, 'til the sun don't_ shine. Sat - is - fy_ your soul be - fore_ los - in' my mind. You'd bet - ter

Chorus:

know it. You'd bet - ter know it 'cause it's me and you. You'd_ bet - ter know it. You'd bet - ter know it this is

Saxes *(arr. for gtr.)*

Cont. rhy. simile

You Better Know It - 5 - 1

251

You Better Know It - 5 - 4

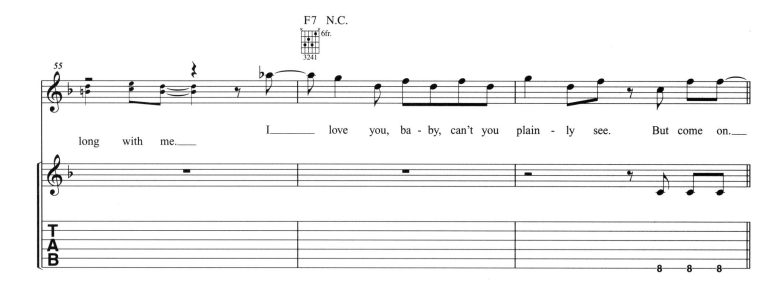

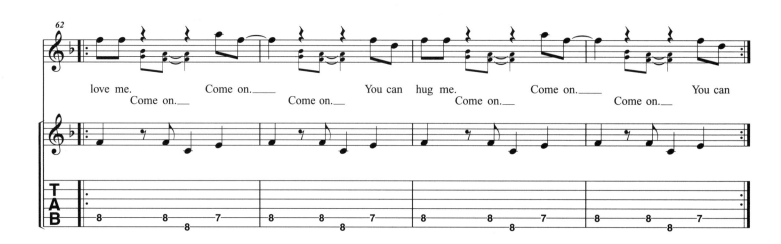

(FOR) YOUR PRECIOUS LOVE

To match recording, tune down 1/2 step:
⑥ = E♭ ♯   ③ = G♭ ♯
⑤ = A♭ ♯   ② = B♭ ♯
④ = D♭ ♯   ① = E♭ ♯

Words and Music by
ARTHUR BROOKS,
RICHARD BROOKS and JERRY BUTLER

Slowly ♩. = **54**
Intro:

*Recording sounds a half step lower than written.

Verse 1:
w/Rhy. Figs. 1 & 1A *(Elec. Gtrs. 1 & 2) 2 times*

Your_____ pre - cious love_____ means_____ more to me_____

(For) Your Precious Love - 3 - 1